$\mathscr{L}$ENT *and* $\mathscr{E}$ASTER $\mathscr{W}$ISDOM

—— *from* ——

SAINT FRANCIS
AND
SAINT CLARE
OF ASSISI

Daily Scripture and Prayers
Together With Saint Francis and
Saint Clare of Assisi's Own Words

Compiled by John V. K

D1407931

Liguori
LIGUORI, MISSOURI

Imprimi Potest:
Thomas D. Picton, C.Ss.R.
Provincial, Denver Province
The Redemptorists

Published by Liguori
Liguori, Missouri
To order, call 800-325-9521
www.liguori.org

Library of Congress Cataloging-in-Publication Data

Lent and Easter wisdom from Saint Francis and Saint Clare of Assisi : daily Scripture and prayers together with Saint Francis and Saint Clare of Assisi's own words / compiled by John V. Kruse. — 1st ed.
  p. cm.
  ISBN 978-0-7648-1765-6
1. Francis, of Assisi, Saint, 1182-1226. 2. Clare, of Assisi, Saint, 1194-1253. 3. Lent. 4. Easter. 5. Devotional literature. I. Francis, of Assisi, Saint, 1182-1226. II. Clare, of Assisi, Saint, 1194-1253. III. Kruse, John V.
  BX4700.F6L453 2008
  242'.34—dc22

2008039674

Printed in the United States of America
First edition
12 11 10 09 08 5 4 3 2 1

Contents

Epigraph

PRAYER FOR A LENTEN JOURNEY

Almighty, eternal, just and merciful God,
give us miserable ones
the grace to do for You alone
what we know you want us to do
and always to desire what pleases You.
Inwardly cleansed,
interiorly enlightened
and inflamed by the fire of the Holy Spirit,
may we be able to follow
in the footprints of Your beloved Son,
our Lord Jesus Christ,
and, by Your grace alone,
may we make our way to You,
Most High,
Who live and rule
in perfect Trinity and simple Unity,
and are glorified
God almighty,
forever and ever.
Amen.

ST. FRANCIS OF ASSISI,
"A LETTER TO THE ENTIRE ORDER," 120-121

Introduction

ALTHOUGH THEY LIVED NEARLY 800 YEARS AGO, St. Francis (1181/2–1226) and St. Clare of Assisi (1194–1253) serve as excellent guides for the modern Lenten journey. Both saints underwent powerful conversion experiences in their lives as they sought the joy and fulfillment that comes from following Christ to the cross and from sharing in the new life of his resurrection. Praying before the crucifix of the dilapidated Church of San Damiano just outside of Assisi, a young Francis heard Christ call him to rebuild his Church. Initially, Francis interpreted this call literally and began rebuilding San Damiano. Eventually Francis understood that Christ was calling him to serve as an agent of reform in the Church in general. Having abandoned the comfortable life of the Italian merchant class, he embraced a life of radical poverty in order to free himself of anything that would hinder him in his quest to live a life of authentic Christian discipleship.

Inspired by the example of Francis and his first followers, Clare, a member of the noble class, left behind everything to establish an expression of the Franciscan vision of Christian discipleship for women. The two saints, who supported each other in their efforts to live humble, simple lives totally dependent on the generosity of God, understood the essence of the paschal mystery: To share in the life of Christ, one also had to die with him. This the saints did through their own lives of poverty, penance, and self-sacrifice. In their existent writings, which are quite meager by modern standards and are composed primarily of prayers, letters, poetry, rules of life, and testaments, Francis and Clare express their vision of the gospel life. Included in these writings are numerous themes extremely appropriate for the Lenten and Easter seasons: penance, conversion, self-sacrifice, service, embracing the cross, the humility and charity of Christ, joy, new life, and mission. May the words and example of these two great saints inspire us to faithfully follow Christ to the cross so that, together with them, we might experience the joy and new life of Easter.

A BRIEF HISTORY OF LENT

Most Catholics seem to be aware that the forty-day period before the feast of Easter—Lent, which comes from the Anglo-Saxon word *lencten*, meaning "spring"—is a time marked by particular rituals, such as the reception of ashes on Ash Wednesday or the decision to "give up French fries." Is Lent broader than just these practices that seem to be left over from another era?

In the first three centuries of Christian experience, preparation for the Easter feast usually covered a period of one or two days, perhaps a week at the most. Saint Irenaeus of Lyons (ca. AD 140–202) even speaks of a *forty-hour* preparation for Easter.

The first reference to Lent as a period of forty days' preparation occurs in the teachings of the First Council of Nicaea in AD 325. By the end of the fourth century, a Lenten period of forty days was established and accepted.

In its early development, Lent quickly became associated with the sacrament of baptism, since Easter was the great baptismal feast. Those who were preparing to be baptized participated in the season of Lent in preparation for the reception of the sacrament of baptism. Eventually, those who were already baptized considered it important to join these candidates preparing for baptism in their preparations for Easter. The customs and practices of Lent as we know them today soon took hold.

LENT AS A JOURNEY

Lent is often portrayed as a journey, from one point in time to another point in time. The concept of journey is obvious for those experiencing the Rite of Christian Initiation of Adults (RCIA), the program of baptismal preparation conducted in most parishes during the season of Lent.

But Lenten preparation is not limited to those who are preparing to be baptized and join the Church. For many Catholics, Lent is a journey that is measured from Ash Wednesday through Easter Sunday, but more accurately, Lent is measured from Ash Wednesday to the beginning of the period known as the Triduum.

Triduum begins after the Mass on Holy Thursday, continues through Good Friday, and concludes with the Easter Vigil on Holy Saturday. Lent officially ends with the proclamation of the *Exsultet*, "Rejoice, O Heavenly Powers," during the Mass of Holy Saturday.

By whatever yardstick the journey is measured, it is not only the time that is important but the essential experiences of the journey that are necessary for a full appreciation of what is being celebrated.

The Lenten journey is also a process of spiritual growth and, as such, presumes movement from one state of being to another state. For example, some people may find themselves troubled and anxious at the beginning of Lent as a result of a life choice or an unanswered question, and, at the end of Lent, they may fully expect a sense of conversion, a sense of peace, or perhaps simply understanding and acceptance. Therefore, Lent is a movement from one point of view to another or, perhaps, from one interpretation of life to a different interpretation.

Scripture, psalms, prayers, rituals, practices, and penance are the components of the Lenten journey. Each component, tried and tested by years of tradition, is one of the "engines" that drives the season and which brings the weary spiritual traveler to the joys of Easter.

PENITENTIAL NATURE OF LENT

A popular understanding of Lent is that it is a penitential period of time during which people attempt to become more sensitive to the role of sin in their lives. Lenten sermons will speak of personal sin, coming to an awareness of the sins of others and the effect such sin might have, and the sin that can be found within our larger society and culture. Awareness of sin, however, is balanced by an emphasis on the love and acceptance that God still has for humanity, despite the sinful condition in which we still find ourselves.

The practice of meditation of the Passion of the Lord, his suffering and his death, is also seen as part of the penitential experience of Lent. There is also a traditional concern for the reception of the sacrament of reconciliation during Lent. Originally, the sacrament of reconciliation was celebrated before Lent began. The penance was imposed on Ash Wednesday and performed during the entire forty-day period.

SUMMONS TO PENITENTIAL LIVING

"Jesus came to Galilee, proclaiming the good news of God, and saying, 'The time is fulfilled, and the kingdom of God has come near; repent, and believe in the good news'" (Mark 1:14–15). This call to conversion announces the solemn opening of Lent. Participants are marked with ashes, and the words, "Repent, and believe in the good news," are prayed. This blessing is understood as a personal acceptance of the desire to take on the life of penance for the sake of the gospel.

The example of Jesus in the desert for forty days—a time during which he fasted and prayed—is imitated. It is time to center attention on conversion. During Lent, the expectation is to examine our lives and, through the practice of prayer, fasting, and works of charity, seek to conform our lives to Christ's. For some, this conversion will be a turning from sin to grace. For others, it will be a gracious turning toward the mystery of God in Christ. Whatever the pattern chosen by a particular pilgrim for an observance of Lent, it is hoped that this book will provide a useful support in the effort.

PART I

~~~~~

READINGS *for* LENT

Ash Wednesday

DAY 1

Joining Francis at the Cross: The Beginning of Our Lenten Journey

Most High,
glorious God,
enlighten the darkness of my heart
and give me
true faith,
certain hope,
and perfect charity,
sense and knowledge,
Lord,
that I may carry out
Your holy and true command.

ST. FRANCIS OF ASSISI,
"THE PRAYER BEFORE THE CRUCIFIX," 40

GOING INTO THE WILDERNESS

Then Jesus was led up by the Spirit into the wilderness to be tempted by the devil. He fasted forty days and forty nights, and afterwards he was famished.

MATTHEW 4:1–2

PRAYER

Lord, I ask that you accompany me on my Lenten journey. Open my heart to your will for me. May the journey lead me to soul searching and conversion so that I might experience a deeper relationship with you when I arrive at the celebration of Easter joy.

LENTEN ACTION

Take five extra minutes to pray before a crucifix. What is it that Christ wills for you this Lenten season? Write down three ways that you might become a more faithful follower of Christ. Keep the list in this book for review throughout the season.

Steadfastness

What you hold, may you hold,
What you do, may you do and not stop.
But with swift pace, light step, unswerving feet,
so that even your steps stir up no dust,
may you go forward
securely, joyfully, and swiftly,
on the path of prudent happiness,
believing nothing,
agreeing with nothing
that would dissuade you from this commitment
Ps 50:14 *or would place a stumbling block* for you on the way,
Rom 14:13 so that nothing prevents you from *offering*
your vows to the Most High in the perfection
to which the Spirit of the Lord has called you.

ST. CLARE OF ASSISI,
"THE SECOND LETTER TO AGNES OF PRAGUE," 48*

*Clare wrote a series of letters to Agnes of Prague, the daughter of the King
of Bohemia. Inspired by the life of Clare, Princess Agnes wished to aban-*

don noble life, emulate Clare, and establish a monastery following the life of Clare's Poor Ladies in Prague.

Passages taken from the Scripture are in Italics.

PERSEVERING IN THE LORD

In the presence of God and of Christ Jesus, who is to judge the living and the dead, and in view of his appearing and his kingdom, I solemnly urge you: proclaim the message; be persistent whether the time is favorable or unfavorable; convince, rebuke, and encourage, with the utmost patience in teaching. As for you, always be sober, endure suffering, do the work of an evangelist, carry out your ministry fully. As for me, I am already being poured out as a libation, and the time of my departure has come. I have fought the good fight, I have finished the race, I have kept the faith. From now on there is reserved for me the crown of righteousness, which the Lord, the righteous judge, will give me on that day, and not only to me but also to all who have longed for his appearing.

2 TIMOTHY 4:1–2, 5–8

PRAYER

Lord Jesus, you remained faithful to your Father's will to the point of death. Strengthened by your Spirit, may I remain faithful to you during this Lenten journey as I accompany you on your way to the cross.

LENTEN ACTION

When you find it difficult to follow God's vocation for you today, ask Jesus for the strength to persevere.

DAY 3

Reflecting God's Mercy

I wish to know in this way if you love the Lord and me, His servant and yours: that there is not any brother in the world who has sinned—however much he could have sinned—who, after he has looked into your eyes, would ever depart without your mercy, if he is looking for mercy. And if he were not looking for mercy, you would ask him if he wants mercy. And if he would sin a thousand times before your eyes, love him more than me so that you may draw him to the Lord; and always be merciful with brothers such as these....

ST. FRANCIS OF ASSISI,
"A LETTER TO A MINISTER," 97–98

MERCY BEYOND JUSTICE

Then Jesus said, "There was a man who had two sons. The younger of them said to his father, 'Father, give me the share of the property that will belong to me.' So he divided his property between them. A few days later the younger son gathered all he had and traveled to a distant country, and there he squandered his property in dissolute living. When he had spent everything, a severe famine took place throughout that country, and he began to be in need. So he set off and went to his father. But while he was still far off, his father saw him and was filled with compassion; he ran and put his arms around him and kissed him. Then the son said to him, 'Father, I have sinned against heaven and before you; I am no longer worthy to be called your son.' But the father said to his slaves, 'Quickly, bring out a robe—the best one—and put it on him; put a ring on his finger and sandals on his feet. And get the fatted calf and kill it, and let us eat and celebrate; for this son of mine was dead and is alive again; he was lost and is found!' And they began to celebrate.

LUKE 15:11–14, 20–24

PRAYER

Merciful Lord, I have failed you in many aspects of my life. Yet, you do not require retribution from me. Rather, you reach out to me with unconditional love, and your mercy goes far beyond what human justice might require. Keep me mindful of your mercy toward me so that I might better show mercy toward others.

LENTEN ACTION

When someone wrongs you, rather than demanding that he or she makes up for the offense, demonstrate mercy by letting that person "off of the hook."

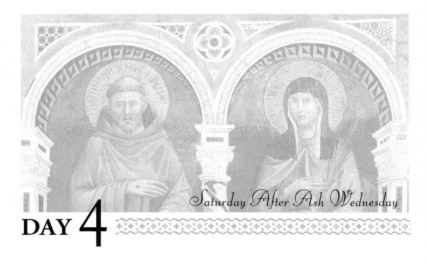

DAY 4

Following the Call

2 Cor 1:3   Among the other gifts that we have received and continue to receive from our magnanimous *Father of mercies* and for which we must express the deepest thanks to our glorious God, there is our vocation, which the more perfect and greater it is, the more

1 Cor 1:26
Jn 14:6;
1 Tm 4:12   are we indebted to Him. Therefore the Apostle [writes]: *Recognize your vocation.* The Son of God has become for us *the Way* that our blessed father Francis, His true lover and imitator, has shown and taught us by word and example.

ST. CLARE OF ASSISI, "THE TESTAMENT," 60

GAINING ONE'S LIFE BY FOLLOWING THE CALL

Then Jesus told his disciples, "If any want to become my follow-
ers, let them deny themselves and take up their cross and follow
me. For those who want to save their life will lose it, and those
who lose their life for my sake will find it. For what will it profit
them if they gain the whole world but forfeit their life?

MATTHEW 16:24–26

PRAYER

Christ, you call us to leave our own will behind and to follow
you. Each of us is called to do this in our own unique way.
This is my own personal call to holiness. This Lenten season,
remind me that I need not be anything more than what you
call me to be. Help me to hear your call, and show me the
path to the life that comes from being your follower.

LENTEN ACTION

Each of us is called to bring Christ to others in our own
particular circumstances in life. This is our unique vocation.
Take time to reflect on just what Christ is calling you to do
with your life, and strive to live out the call more faithfully.

DAY 5

Finding Christ Amidst the Poor, Suffering, and Marginalized

Sir 35:4

The Lord gave me, Brother Francis, thus to begin doing penance in this way: for when I was in sin, it seemed too bitter for me to see lepers. And the Lord Himself led me among them and I showed mercy to them. And when I left them, what had seemed bitter to me was turned into sweetness of soul and body. And afterwards I delayed a little and left the world.

ST. FRANCIS OF ASSISI, "THE TESTAMENT," 124

TO MINISTER TO CHRIST'S PEOPLE IS TO MINISTER TO CHRIST

Then the king will say to those at his right hand, "Come, you that are blessed by my Father, inherit the kingdom prepared for you from the foundation of the world; for I was hungry and you gave me food, I was thirsty and you gave me something to drink, I was a stranger and you welcomed me, I was naked and you gave me clothing, I was sick and you took care of me, I was in prison and you visited me." Then the righteous will answer him, "Lord, when was it that we saw you hungry and gave you food, or thirsty and gave you something to drink? And when was it that we saw you a stranger and welcomed you, or naked and gave you clothing? And when was it that we saw you sick or in prison and visited you?" And the king will answer them, "Truly I tell you, just as you did it to one of the least of these who are members of my family, you did it to me."

MATTHEW 25:34–40

PRAYER

Christ, you humbled yourself by assuming our humanity. You did not become a powerful earthly king, but rather associated with the poor, sick, and outcasts of your day. During this Lenten season, remind me that in my own world, you are not to be found in the thrones of power but amidst the suffering of the lowly. Enlighten and strengthen me as I seek to reach out to those who are forgotten and excluded in our society. Lead me to recognize that in serving them, I am in fact serving you.

LENTEN ACTION

Early in his life, Francis was repulsed by lepers, but he eventually came to see Christ in their faces. From whom do you turn away in your own life? Take a step to reach out to include this person or group of people.

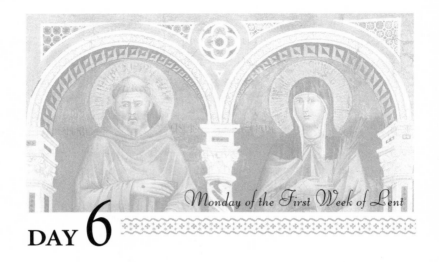

DAY 6

Burning with Love for Christ

…[M]ay you, therefore, be inflamed ever more strongly with the fire of love! As you further contemplate His ineffable delights, riches and perpetual honors, and, sighing, may you cry out from the great desire and love of your heart:

Ct 1:3 *"Draw me after you,*
       let us run in the fragrance of your perfumes,
       O heavenly Spouse!
Ct 2:4 I will run and not tire,
       until *You bring me into the wine-cellar,*
       until Your *left hand is under my head*
Ct 2:6 and Your *right hand will embrace me* happily,
Ct 1:1 *You will kiss me with the* happiest *kiss of Your mouth."*

ST. CLARE OF ASSISI,
"THE FOURTH LETTER TO AGNES OF PRAGUE," 57

LET YOUR FLAME SHINE

"You are the salt of the earth; but if salt has lost its taste, how can its saltiness be restored? It is no longer good for anything, but is thrown out and trampled under foot.

"You are the light of the world. A city built on a hill cannot be hid. No one after lighting a lamp puts it under the bushel basket, but on the lampstand, and it gives light to all in the house. In the same way, let your light shine before others, so that they may see your good works and give glory to your Father in heaven.

MATTHEW 5:13–16

PRAYER

Lord Jesus, the love I share with others in this world is only a small reflection of your love for me. It is a spark compared with the light of the sun. This Lenten season, enkindle my heart so that the fire of my own love for you might grow in intensity and better resemble your love for me. May my life itself be a flame that makes your own light present in the world.

LENTEN ACTION

Use a candle during prayer this Lenten season as a reminder of the love of Christ that burns within you. Be an agent of light in a world that often seems overcome by darkness; be a positive and uplifting presence to those around you.

Tuesday of the First Week of Lent

DAY 7

Christk's Continued Presence With Us

As He revealed Himself to the holy apostles in true flesh, so He reveals Himself to us now in sacred bread. And as they saw only His flesh by an insight of their flesh, yet believed that He was God as they contemplated Him with their spiritual eyes, let us, as we see bread and wine with our bodily eyes, see and firmly believe that they are His most holy Body and Blood living and true. And in this way the Lord is always with His faithful, as He Himself says:

Mt 28:20 *Behold I am with you until the end of the age.*

ST. FRANCIS OF ASSISI, *THE ADMONITIONS*
(I: THE BODY OF CHRIST), 129

Remembering

For I received from the Lord what I also handed on to you, that the Lord Jesus on the night when he was betrayed took a loaf of bread, and when he had given thanks, he broke it and said, "This is my body that is for you. Do this in remembrance of me." In the same way he took the cup also, after supper, saying, "This cup is the new covenant in my blood. Do this, as often as you drink it, in remembrance of me." For as often as you eat this bread and drink the cup, you proclaim the Lord's death until he comes.

1 Corinthians 11:23–26

Prayer

Lord, during your earthly life you gathered people to you by sharing a meal with them. You continue to draw me to you through the meal in which you give your very self to me. I thank you for this nourishment that strengthens me for my spiritual journey and unites me with you and others. May I never lose sight of the significance of this great gift.

Lenten Action

During this Lenten season, make a concerted effort to pray to Christ in the presence of the Blessed Sacrament.

DAY 8

Controlling One's Tongue

*L*et [the sisters] conduct themselves virtuously and say little, so that those who see them may always be edified….Let them not presume to repeat the gossip of the world inside the monastery. Let them be strictly bound not to repeat outside the monastery anything that is said or done within which could cause scandal.

ST. CLARE OF ASSISI, *THE FORM OF LIFE OF SAINT CLARE* (IX: THE PENANCE TO BE IMPOSED ON THE SISTERS WHO SIN; THE SISTERS WHO SERVE OUTSIDE THE MONASTERY), 122

Using Words to Draw Near to God

O LORD, who may abide in your tent?
Who may dwell on your holy hill?

Those who walk blamelessly, and do what is right,
* and speak the truth from their heart;*
who do not slander with their tongue,
* and do no evil to their friends,*
* nor take up a reproach against their neighbors;*
in whose eyes the wicked are despised,
* but who honor those who fear the LORD;*
* who stand by their oath even to their hurt;...*

Those who do these things shall never be moved.

PSALM 15:1–5

Prayer

Lord Jesus, from experience I know that the tongue is a powerful weapon that can be used for good or bad. This Lent, give me the gift of your Spirit so that I may be discerning in my choice of words and use them to build up and not to tear down others.

Lenten Action

When tempted to say something negative about someone today, even if the negative information is true, hold your tongue.

DAY 9

Christ, Source of Our Strength

Let *every creature*
in heaven, on earth, in the sea and in the depths,
give praise, *glory, honor and blessing*
To Him Who suffered so much,
Who has given and will give in the future every good,
for He is our power and strength,
Who *alone is good,*
Who alone is almighty,
Who alone is omnipotent, wonderful, glorious
and Who alone is holy,
worthy of praise and blessing
through endless ages.
Amen.

ST. FRANCIS OF ASSISI, "LATER ADMONITION AND EXHORTATION
TO THE BROTHERS AND SISTERS OF PENANCE," 49–50

Rv 5:13

GOD'S ARMOR

Therefore take up the whole armor of God, so that you may be able to withstand on that evil day, and having done everything, to stand firm. Stand therefore, and fasten the belt of truth around your waist, and put on the breastplate of righteousness. As shoes for your feet put on whatever will make you ready to proclaim the gospel of peace. With all of these, take the shield of faith, with which you will be able to quench all the flaming arrows of the evil one. Take the helmet of salvation, and the sword of the Spirit, which is the word of God.

Pray in the Spirit at all times in every prayer and supplication. To that end keep alert and always persevere in supplication for all the saints.

EPHESIANS 6:13–18

PRAYER

Lord, you alone can provide me with the strength to confront the many forces in the world that seek to beat me down and direct me away from you. Be my strength when I am weak, when I think I can no longer go on.

LENTEN ACTION

Go for a walk or do some other form of exercise. While exercising, be mindful of the strength that God gives you as you face challenges and temptations in life.

DAY 10

The Blessings of Detachment
from Material Things

O blessed poverty,
who bestows eternal riches
on those who love and embrace her!
O holy poverty,
God promises the kingdom of heaven
and, beyond any doubt, reveals eternal glory
and blessed life to those who have and desire her!
O God-centered poverty,
whom the Lord Jesus Christ
Who ruled and still rules heaven and earth,
Ps 32:9; 148:5   Who spoke and things were made,
came down to embrace before all else!

ST. CLARE OF ASSISI,
"THE FIRST LETTER TO AGNES OF PRAGUE," 45

WHERE IS YOUR TREASURE?

"Do not store up for yourselves treasures on earth, where moth and rust consume and where thieves break in and steal; but store up for yourselves treasures in heaven, where neither moth nor rust consumes and where thieves do not break in and steal. For where your treasure is, there your heart will be also....."No one can serve two masters; for a slave will either hate the one and love the other, or be devoted to the one and despise the other. You cannot serve God and wealth.

MATTHEW 6:19–21, 24

PRAYER

Jesus, my Lord, our culture tells me that the accumulation of material goods will bring me happiness. You tell me differently. Through your own life, you have shown me how detachment from material goods allows one to recognize the genuine satisfaction of giving oneself in loving service to others. Free me from the compulsion to have things, and help me to recognize, along with Francis and Clare, that all I really need is you.

LENTEN ACTION

Be aware of the consumerist mentality that surrounds all of us. Resist impulse buying and devote time to those things that bring genuine satisfaction in your life, such as prayer, relationships, and assisting others.

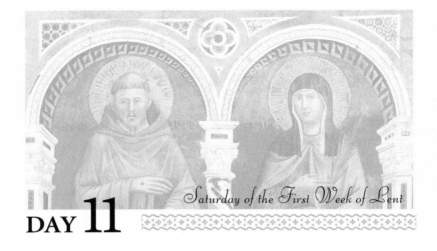

Family

Mt 12:50;
Mk 3:35

1 Cor 6:20

Mt 5:16

We are spouses when the faithful soul is united by the Holy Spirit to our Lord Jesus Christ. We are brothers, moreover, when we do *the will of* His *Father Who* is in heaven; mothers when we carry Him in our heart and body through love and a pure and sincere conscience; and give Him birth through a holy activity, which must shine before others by example.

ST. FRANCIS OF ASSISI, "LATER ADMONITION AND EXHORTATION
TO THE BROTHERS AND SISTERS OF PENANCE," 49

THE LOVE OF CHRIST IN GOD'S FAMILY

For this reason I bow my knees before the Father, from whom every family in heaven and on earth takes its name. I pray that, according to the riches of his glory, he may grant that you may be strengthened in your inner being with power through his Spirit, and that Christ may dwell in your hearts through faith, as you are being rooted and grounded in love. I pray that you may have the power to comprehend, with all the saints, what is the breadth and length and height and depth, and to know the love of Christ that surpasses knowledge, so that you may be filled with all the fullness of God.

Now to him who by the power at work within us is able to accomplish abundantly far more than all we can ask or imagine, to him be glory in the church and in Christ Jesus to all generations, forever and ever. Amen.

EPHESIANS 3:14–21

PRAYER

Christ, I thank you for the gift of my physical family, yet I realize that my relationship with you is deeper than any other relationship that I can have. Help me to deepen that relationship by filling me with your Spirit. Strengthen me to do your Father's will. Purify my heart and be with me as I strive to make you present in the world through my loving actions. I ask you, Lord, to bless members of my earthly family, those with whom I am close as well as those with whom I may be estranged.

LENTEN ACTION

Francis states that one way we make Christ present in the world is through acting on a pure conscience. Examine your conscience as regards your relationships with family members. Work at improving or healing a familial relationship.

DAY 12

Becoming Perfect by Following in the Loving Footprints of the Groom

*T*his is that perfection with which that King will join you to Himself in the heavenly bridal chamber where He is seated in glory on a starry throne, because you have despised the splendor of an earthly kingdom and considered of little value the offers of an imperial marriage.* Instead, as someone zealous for the holiest poverty, in a spirit of great humility and the most ardent love, you have held fast *to the footprints* of Him to Whom you merited to be joined in marriage.

1 Pt 2:21

ST. CLARE OF ASSISI,
"THE SECOND LETTER TO AGNES OF PRAGUE," 47

Emperor Frederick II had offered marriage to Agnes.

PERFECTION IN LOVE

"You have heard that it was said, 'You shall love your neighbor and hate your enemy.' But I say to you, Love your enemies and pray for those who persecute you, so that you may be children of your Father in heaven; for he makes his sun rise on the evil and on the good, and sends rain on the righteous and on the unrighteous. For if you love those who love you, what reward do you have? Do not even the tax collectors do the same? And if you greet only your brothers and sisters, what more are you doing than others? Do not even the Gentiles do the same? Be perfect, therefore, as your heavenly Father is perfect.

MATTHEW 5:43–48

PRAYER

Lord Jesus, it can be easy to love my friends and family, but you call me to love even my enemies. Help me to follow in your footsteps and to learn not to respond to hatred with hatred and to violence with violence. Fill my heart with your own perfect love so that I can love even when it is most difficult.

LENTEN ACTION

Reflect Christ's perfect love in the world. When someone angers you, hurts you, or annoys you, respond in love with a kind word or a favor.

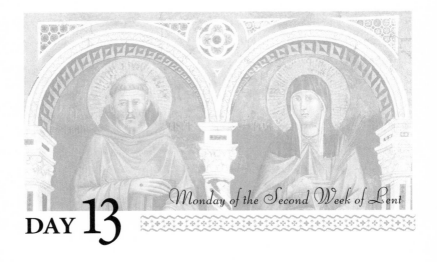

DAY 13

Becoming Vulnerable in Order to Do God's Work

*W*herever they may be, let all my brothers remember that they have given themselves and abandoned their bodies to the Lord Jesus Christ. For love of Him, they must make themselves vulnerable to their enemies, both visible and invisible, because the Lord says: *Whoever loses his life because of me will save it* in eternal life. *Blessed are they who suffer persecution for the sake of justice, for theirs is the kingdom of heaven. If they have persecuted me, they will also persecute you. If they persecute you in one town, flee to another. Blessed are you when people hate you, speak evil of you, persecute, expel, and abuse you, denounce your name as evil and utter every kind of slander against you because of me. Rejoice and be glad on that day because your reward is great in heaven.*

Lk 9:24;
Mt 25:46

Mt 5:10

Jn 15:20

Mt 10:23;
Mt 5:11; Lk 6:22

Mt 5:11

Lk 6:22; Mt 5:11

Lk 6:23; Mt 5:12

ST. FRANCIS OF ASSISI, *THE EARLIER RULE* (XVI: THOSE GOING AMONG THE SARACENS AND OTHER NONBELIEVERS), 74–75

Taking the Risk of Extending Oneself for Others

Just then a lawyer stood up to test Jesus. "Teacher," he said, "what must I do to inherit eternal life?" He said to him, "What is written in the law? What do you read there?" He answered, "You shall love the Lord your God with all your heart, and with all your soul, and with all your strength, and with all your mind; and your neighbor as yourself." And he said to him, "You have given the right answer; do this, and you will live."

But wanting to justify himself, he asked Jesus, "And who is my neighbor?" Jesus replied, "A man was going down from Jerusalem to Jericho, and fell into the hands of robbers, who stripped him, beat him, and went away, leaving him half dead. Now by chance a priest was going down that road; and when he saw him, he passed by on the other side. So likewise a Levite, when he came to the place and saw him, passed by on the other side. But a Samaritan while traveling came near him; and when he saw him, he was moved with pity. He went to him and bandaged his wounds, having poured oil and wine on them. Then he put him on his own animal, brought him to an inn, and took care of him. The next day he took out two denarii, gave them to the innkeeper, and said, 'Take care of him; and when I come back, I will repay you whatever more you spend.' Which of these three, do you think, was a neighbor to the man who fell into the hands of the robbers?" He said, "The one who showed him mercy." Jesus said to him, "Go and do likewise."

LUKE 10:25–37

Prayer

Lord, as you found out in your own life, when I try to do good for others, I can often end up getting wounded myself. Yet, you continue to call me to trust in you and to extend myself for others. May the knowledge that comes from knowing that I am striving to do your will, even when I feel wounded by opening myself to others, give me the strength and courage to continue to serve you.

LENTEN ACTION

As the saying goes, no good deed goes unpunished. In spite of the hesitancy that this sentiment may inspire, trust in God. Extend yourself for the good of another today, even if your good deed may be turned against you and result in you feeling wounded.

DAY 14

The Ultimate Humility of Christ

...embrace the poor Christ.
Look upon Him Who became contemptible for you,
and follow Him, making yourself contemptible in this
world
for Him.
...gaze,
consider,
contemplate
desiring to imitate...,

[Who] though more beautiful than the children of men became, for Ps 119:32
your salvation, the lowest of men, *was despised, struck, scourged* Ps 45:3
untold times throughout His entire body, and then died amid the
suffering of the Cross.

ST. CLARE OF ASSISI,
"THE SECOND LETTER TO AGNES OF PRAGUE," 49

HUMILITY DEMONSTRATED BY GREAT SACRIFICE

Let the same mind be in you that was in Christ Jesus,
who, though he was in the form of God,
did not regard equality with God
as something to be exploited,
but emptied himself,
taking the form of a slave,
being born in human likeness.
And being found in human form,
he humbled himself
and became obedient to the point of death—
even death on a cross.

Therefore God also highly exalted him
and gave him the name
that is above every name,
so that at the name of Jesus
every knee should bend,
in heaven and on earth and under the earth,
and every tongue should confess
that Jesus Christ is Lord,
to the glory of God the Father.

PHILIPPIANS 2:5–11

PRAYER

Christ, it is difficult for me to even begin contemplate your great humility. You humbled yourself by becoming human and by dying an ignominious death for the sake of others. Inspired by your own example of humility, lead me to greater humility so that I can be better able to discover you and grow in my relationship with you. As I do so, show me the blessings that are to be found in placing my own interests aside and in giving of myself in the service of others.

LENTEN ACTION

Take five minutes to reflect on the humility of Christ. What are some of the ways Christ demonstrated his humility? What does this humility tell you about his love for you? Practice emulating Christ's humility by letting go of your own wishes and deferring to the preferences of others.

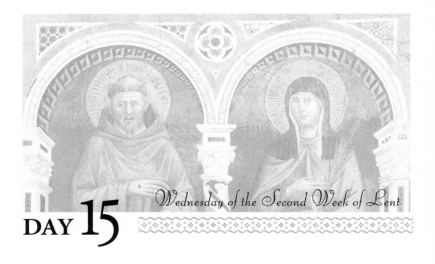

DAY 15

Generosity and the Multiplication of Blessings

lms are a legacy and a justice due to the poor that our Lord Jesus Christ acquired for us. The brothers who work at acquiring them will receive a great reward and enable those who give them to gain and acquire one; for all that people leave behind in the world will perish, but they will have a reward from the Lord for the charity and almsgiving they have done.

ST. FRANCIS OF ASSISI,
THE EARLIER RULE (IX: BEGGING ALMS), 71

GENEROSITY FROM THE HEART

We want you to know, brothers and sisters, about the grace of God that has been granted to the churches of Macedonia; for during a severe ordeal of affliction, their abundant joy and their extreme poverty have overflowed in a wealth of generosity on their part. For, as I can testify, they voluntarily gave according to their means, and even beyond their means, begging us earnestly for the privilege of sharing in this ministry to the saints— and this, not merely as we expected; they gave themselves first to the Lord and, by the will of God, to us…

2 CORINTHIANS 8:1–5

PRAYER

God of all generosity, you have abundantly poured your love into the world as is evidenced by the many gifts around me, especially the gift of your own Son. May I seek always to reflect your own generosity by giving to others, even when such giving impinges upon me in some way.

LENTEN ACTION

One aspect of Lent and the lives of Francis and Clare is letting go of things and placing trust in God. Take a practical step to give of your time, talents, or financial resources to those in need. Trust in God's care for you, and don't just give of your excess. Give of yourself, even to the point of sacrifice.

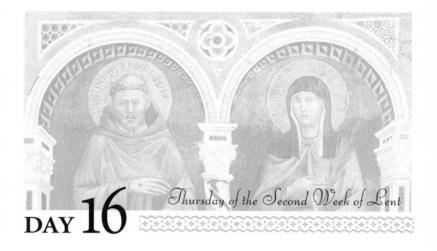

DAY 16

Uniting Our Sufferings
With Christ's Own Sufferings

Rom 8:17;
Tm 2:12

1 Cor 12:26

Ps 110:3

Phil 4:3; Rv 3:5

If you suffer with Him, you will reign with Him.
weeping with Him, you will rejoice with Him;
dying on the cross of tribulation *with Him,*
you will possess heavenly mansions with Him
among the splendor of the saints
and *in the Book of Life* your *name* will be called glorious
among the peoples.

ST. CLARE OF ASSISI,
"THE SECOND LETTER TO AGNES OF PRAGUE," 49

GROWTH THROUGH SUFFERING

Therefore, since we are justified by faith, we have peace with God through our Lord Jesus Christ, through whom we have obtained access to this grace in which we stand; and we boast in our hope of sharing the glory of God. And not only that, but we also boast in our sufferings, knowing that suffering produces endurance, and endurance produces character, and character produces hope, and hope does not disappoint us, because God's love has been poured into our hearts through the Holy Spirit that has been given to us.

ROMANS 5:1–5

PRAYER

Lord Jesus, you did not avoid suffering. With great faith in your Father, you faced it head-on. I live in a world that urges me to avoid suffering at all costs. Give me strength as I too face suffering in life. Help me to remember that suffering is part of the growth process of becoming the kind of person who is suited to spend eternal life with you.

LENTEN ACTION

Today, tackle the task you have been putting off for fear of suffering. Unite any suffering you experience today with Christ's own redemptive suffering.

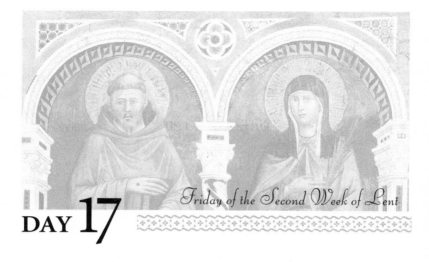

Freedom in Christ

All those, however, who are not living in penance, who do not receive he Body and Blood of our Lord Jesus Christ, who practice vice and sin and walk after evil concupiscence and wicked desires, who do not observe what they have promised, and who serve the world with their bodies, the desires of the flesh, the cares and anxieties of this world, and the preoccupations of this life [all _{Jn 8:41} these] are deceived by the devil whose children they are and whose works they do. They are blind because they do not see the true light, our Lord Jesus Christ. They do not have spiritual wisdom because they do not possess the Son of God, the true wisdom of the Father, _{Ps 107:27} within them. It is said of them: *Their wisdom has been swallowed up.* They see, recognize, know, and do evil; and, knowingly, they lose their souls.

ST. FRANCIS OF ASSISI, "LATER ADMONITION AND EXHORTATION TO THE BROTHERS AND SISTERS OF PENANCE," 50

THE TRUTH OF CHRIST'S AS THE WAY TO FREEDOM

Then Jesus said to the Jews who had believed in him, "If you continue in my word, you are truly my disciples; and you will know the truth, and the truth will make you free."

JOHN 8:31–32

And you know the way to the place where I am going." Thomas said to him, "Lord, we do not know where you are going. How can we know the way?" Jesus said to him, "I am the way, and the truth, and the life. No one comes to the Father except through me.

JOHN 14:4–6

PRAYER

Lord Jesus, while our society tells us that freedom means doing whatever we want, you tell us that the way to genuine freedom is by following you, the Truth. Guide me with your Holy Spirit so that I may faithfully discern the messages that surround me. Lead me to the freedom you promise by showing me your truth and by helping me always to devote my life to what is good and worthy of my dignity.

LENTEN ACTION

Be especially conscious of the messages you receive from the media. Do these messages reflect the truth of Christ, or do they lead you away from the authentic freedom that Christ offers?

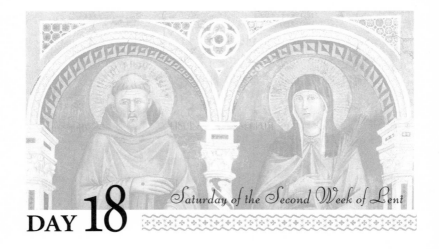

DAY 18

God's Self-Revelation in Love

Place your mind before the mirror of eternity!

Place your soul *in the brilliance of glory!*

Place your heart *in the figure of the* divine *substance*
and, through contemplation,
transform your entire being *into the image*
of the Godhead Itself,
so that you too may feel what friends feel
in tasting *the hidden sweetness*
that, from the beginning,
God Himself has reserved for His lovers.

And, after all who ensnare their blind lovers
in a deceitful and turbulent world
have been completely passed over,
may you totally love Him
Who gave Himself totally for your love,
At Whose beauty the sun and the moon marvel,
Whose rewards and their uniqueness and
grandeur have no limits;

Heb 1:3

2 Cor 3:18

Ps 31:20;
1 Cor 2:9

I am speaking of Him,
the Son of the Most High, …

St. Clare of Assisi,
"The Third Letter to Agnes of Prague," 51

Christ's Eternal Love that Fills Us With the Presence of God

I pray that, according to the riches of his glory, he may grant that you may be strengthened in your inner being with power through his Spirit, and that Christ may dwell in your hearts through faith, as you are being rooted and grounded in love. I pray that you may have the power to comprehend, with all the saints, what is the breadth and length and height and depth, and to know the love of Christ that surpasses knowledge, so that you may be filled with all the fullness of God.

Now to him who by the power at work within us is able to accomplish abundantly far more than all we can ask or imagine, to him be glory in the church and in Christ Jesus to all generations, forever and ever. Amen.

Ephesians 3:16–21

Prayer

Our Lord, you are not a distant god. Rather, you loved us so much that you drew near to us by becoming one of us. You revealed yourself to us through the gift of your Son two thousand years ago, and you continue to reveal yourself to us in the loving union and friendship we share with him today. Be near to us. Show yourself to us. Fill us with your love.

Lenten Action

Spend time with or contact a friend, perhaps one with whom you may have fallen out of touch. Reflect upon how close God is to you and how God's friendship with and love for you is deeper than any friendship or love that you can experience in your earthly life.

DAY 19

Christ, the Good Shepherd

*O*how glorious it is to have a holy and great Father in heaven! O how holy, consoling to have such a beautiful and wonderful Spouse! O how holy and how loving, gratifying, humbling, peace-giving, sweet, worthy of love, and, above all things, desirable: to have such a Brother and such a Son, our Lord Jesus Christ, Who laid down His life for His sheep and prayed to His Father, saying:

Jn 10;15

Holy Father, in your name, save those • whom you have given me in the world; they were yours and you gave them to me. • The words that you gave to me I have given to them, and they accepted them and have believed *in truth that I have come from you and* they have known *that you have sent me….*

Jn 17:11; •Jn17:6

•Jn 17:8

I wish, Father, that where I am, they also may be with me that they may see my glory • in your kingdom. Amen.

Jn 17:24

•Mt 20:21

ST. FRANCIS OF ASSISI, *EARLIER EXHORTATION TO THE BROTHERS AND SISTERS OF PENANCE* (I: THOSE WHO DO PENANCE), 42

Let all of us, brothers, consider the Good Shepherd Who bore the suffering of the cross to save His sheep.

The Lord's sheep followed Him in tribulation and persecution, in shame and hunger, in weakness and temptation, and in other ways; and for these things they received eternal life from the Lord.

ST. FRANCIS OF ASSISI, *THE ADMONITIONS*
(VI: IMITATION OF CHRIST), 131

THE SHEPHERD'S DEVOTION TO HIS SHEEP

What do you think? If a shepherd has a hundred sheep, and one of them has gone astray, does he not leave the ninety-nine on the mountains and go in search of the one that went astray? And if he finds it, truly I tell you, he rejoices over it more than over the ninety-nine that never went astray. So it is not the will of your Father in heaven that one of these little ones should be lost.

MATTHEW 18:12–14

"I am the good shepherd. The good shepherd lays down his life for the sheep.

JOHN 10:11

PRAYER

Lord, my Shepherd, I know that sometimes I stray from you. This Lenten season, I seek to follow you more closely. My path in life can be unclear. There are many false shepherds in the world who seek to lead me in ways different from your own. Yet these shepherds do not care for me as you do. Their ways do not lead to true life. When I am lost, when I am confused, when I stray from you, seek me out and shepherd me, Lord.

LENTEN ACTIVITY

Examine your life for the presence of false shepherds who seek to lead you from the path of Christ. Vow not to give ear to these false shepherds in the future.

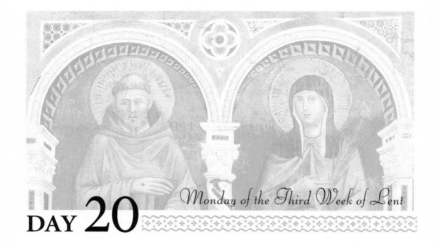

DAY 20

The Wonder of the Human Individual

*I*ndeed, it is now clear that the soul of a faithful person, the most worthy of all creatures because of the grace of God, is greater than heaven itself, since the heavens and the rest of creation cannot contain their Creator; only a faithful soul is His dwelling place and throne, and this only through the charity that the wicked lack. The Truth says: *Whoever loves me will be loved by My Father, and I too shall love him, and We shall come to him and make Our dwelling place with him.*

Jn 14:21, 23

ST. CLARE OF ASSISI,
"THE THIRD LETTER TO AGNES OF PRAGUE," 52

I AM WONDERFULLY MADE

> *O LORD, you have searched me and known me.*
> *You know when I sit down and when I rise up;*
> *you discern my thoughts from far away.*
> *You search out my path and my lying down,*
> *and are acquainted with all my ways.*
> *Even before a word is on my tongue,*
> *O LORD, you know it completely.*

You hem me in, behind and before,
and lay your hand upon me.
Such knowledge is too wonderful for me;
it is so high that I cannot attain it.

Where can I go from your spirit?
Or where can I flee from your presence?
If I ascend to heaven, you are there;
if I make my bed in Sheol, you are there.
If I take the wings of the morning
and settle at the farthest limits of the sea,
even there your hand shall lead me,
and your right hand shall hold me fast.
For it was you who formed my inward parts;
you knit me together in my mother's womb.
I praise you, for I am fearfully and wonderfully made.
Wonderful are your works;
that I know very well.
My frame was not hidden from you,
when I was being made in secret,
intricately woven in the depths of the earth.

PSALM 139:1–10, 13–15

PRAYER

Creator of the universe, you have made me in your own image and likeness. This alone demonstrates my deep connection to you and endows me and all other people with special value and dignity. This Lenten season, remind me of how precious I am in your eyes, and keep me ever mindful of my own dignity and worth as well as that of others.

LENTEN ACTION

Treat all those with whom you come into contact today with the respect that is worthy of their dignity.

DAY 21

Love in Action

I admonish and exhort in the Lord Jesus Christ all my sisters, both those present and those to come, to strive always to imitate the way of holy simplicity, humility and poverty and also the integrity of our holy way of living, as we were taught from the beginning of our conversion by Christ and by our blessed father Francis....And loving one another with the love of Christ, may you demonstrate without in your deeds the love you have within so that, compelled by such an example, the sisters may always grow in the love of God and in mutual charity.

Jas 2:18

ST. CLARE OF ASSISI, "THE TESTAMENT," 64

LOVE IN TRUTH AND ACTION

We know that we have passed from death to life because we love one another. Whoever does not love abides in death. All who hate a brother or sister are murderers, and you know that murderers do not have eternal life abiding in them. We know love by this, that he laid down his life for us—and we ought to lay down our lives for one another. How does God's love abide in anyone who has the world's goods and sees a brother or sister in need and yet refuses help?

Little children, let us love, not in word or speech, but in truth and action. And by this we will know that we are from the truth and will reassure our hearts before him whenever our hearts condemn us; for God is greater than our hearts, and he knows everything.

1 JOHN 3:14–20

PRAYER

Lord, it is easy to have feelings of love in my heart or to say that I have love with my words. However, you ask me to follow your own example by demonstrating my love in my actions. As an important part of my conversion and as a reflection of your own self-giving love, help me to give of myself in loving service to others, in particular to those most in need.

LENTEN ACTION

Often, we do not let those whom we love know it. Let someone know that you love him or her by verbalizing your love and by demonstrating that affection with a loving gesture. Demonstrate your love for our disadvantaged brothers and sisters by volunteering for a social service agency.

The "S-Word": Consequences of Sin

*A*s often as *they have turned away from the commands of the Lord* and "wandered outside obedience" (Honorius III), let all the brothers know, as the Prophet says, they are cursed outside

Ps 119:21 obedience as long as they knowingly remain in such a sin. When they have persevered in the Lord's commands—as they have promised by the Holy Gospel and their life, let them know they have remained in true obedience and are blessed by the Lord.

ST. FRANCIS OF ASSISI, *THE EARLIER RULE*
(V: THE CORRECTION OF THE BROTHERS AT FAULT), 68

From Death to Life

Do you not know that all of us who have been baptized into Christ Jesus were baptized into his death? Therefore we have been buried with him by baptism into death, so that, just as Christ was raised from the dead by the glory of the Father, so we too might walk in newness of life.

For if we have been united with him in a death like his, we will certainly be united with him in a resurrection like his. We know that our old self was crucified with him so that the body of sin might be destroyed, and we might no longer be enslaved to sin. For whoever has died is freed from sin. But if we have died with Christ, we believe that we will also live with him. We know that Christ, being raised from the dead, will never die again; death no longer has dominion over him. The death he died, he died to sin, once for all; but the life he lives, he lives to God. So you also must consider yourselves dead to sin and alive to God in Christ Jesus.

Romans 6:3–11

Prayer

Lord, you call me to follow you because you want what is best for me in life. Yet, sometimes I turn away from you and then suffer the consequences of having rejected your life and love. When I choose darkness and death, call me back to your light and life. I ask for forgiveness for the times I have hurt my relationship with you.

Lenten Action

Remember that sin hurts your relationship with God, with others, and even with yourself. Reflect honestly upon the consequences of sin in your life. Strive to be more faithful to God so as to embrace the life and love that he offers and avoid the consequences of sin. Take a step to heal a wounded relationship in your life.

DAY 23

Conversion Through Acts of Penance

Fear and honor,
praise and bless,

1 Thess 5:18 *give thanks* and adore
the Lord God Almighty in Trinity and in Unity,
Father, Son, and Holy Spirit,
the Creator of all.

Mt 3:2 Do penance,

Lk 3:8 performing worthy fruits of penance
because we shall soon die.

Lk 6:38 *Give and it will be given to you.*

Lk 6:14 *Forgive and you shall be forgiven.*
If you do not forgive people their sins,

Mk 11:25 the Lord *will not forgive you yours.*

Jas 5:16 *Confess all your sins.*
Blessed are those who die in penance,
for they shall be in the kingdom of heaven.
Woe to those who do not die in penance,

1 Jn 3:10 for they shall be *children of the devil*

Jn 8:41 whose works they do

and they shall go *into everlasting fire.* Mt 18:8; 25:41
Beware of and abstain from every evil
and persevere in good till the end.

ST. FRANCIS OF ASSISI, *THE EARLIER RULE* (XXI: THE PRAISE AND
EXHORTATION THAT ALL THE BROTHERS CAN MAKE), 78

TURNING TO THE LORD

*I have sent to you all my servants the prophets, sending them
persistently, saying, 'Turn now everyone of you from your evil
way, and amend your doings, and do not go after other gods
to serve them, and then you shall live in the land that I gave
to you and your ancestors.' But you did not incline your ear or
obey me.*

JEREMIAH 35:15

*Turn to me and be saved,
all the ends of the earth!
For I am God, and there is no other.
By myself I have sworn,
from my mouth has gone forth in righteousness
a word that shall not return:
"To me every knee shall bow,
every tongue shall swear."
Only in the LORD, it shall be said of me,
are righteousness and strength;
all who were incensed against him
shall come to him and be ashamed.
In the LORD all the offspring of Israel
shall triumph and glory.*

ISAIAH 45:22–25

PRAYER

Lord, this Lent I hear you calling me to turn toward you, the source of true life, and away from the "dead-end" of my old way of life. May the acts of penance and self-sacrifice I perform during this holy season serve not as a cause of self-satisfaction and pride, but be means by which I am reminded of my spiritual hunger for you. Turn me to you, Lord.

LENTEN ACTION

Skip a snack or some other pleasurable activity today. Reflect upon your spiritual hunger for God and on the plight of the less-advantaged in the world.

DAY 24

Becoming Christ-Bearers by Following Mary

As the glorious virgin of virgins carried [Him] materially, so you, too, *by following in* her *footprints*, especially [those] of humility and poverty, can, without any doubt, always carry Him spiritually in your chaste and virginal body, holding Him by Whom you and *all things are held together* possessing that which, in comparison with the other transitory possessions of this world you will possess more securely. In this, certain worldly kings and queens are deceived, for, even though their *pride may reach the skies and their heads touch the clouds, in the end they are as forgotten as a dung-heap!*

1 Pet 2:21

Wis 1:7

Is 14:11-15

St. Clare of Assisi,
"The Third Letter to Agnes of Prague," 52

MARY'S FAITHFULNESS

...Meanwhile, standing near the cross of Jesus were his mother, and his mother's sister, Mary the wife of Clopas, and Mary Magdalene. When Jesus saw his mother and the disciple whom he loved standing beside her, he said to his mother, "Woman, here is your son." Then he said to the disciple, "Here is your mother." And from that hour the disciple took her into his own home.

After this, when Jesus knew that all was now finished, he said (in order to fulfill the scripture), "I am thirsty." A jar full of sour wine was standing there. So they put a sponge full of the wine on a branch of hyssop and held it to his mouth. When Jesus had received the wine, he said, "It is finished." Then he bowed his head and gave up his spirit.

JOHN 19:25–30

PRAYER

Mary, my Mother and the Mother of my Lord, this Lenten season teach me by your example. Help me to be open to the will of God as you were throughout your life. Teach me what it means to be a faithful follower of your Son, even to the cross. As I seek to follow in your footsteps as the model of Christian discipleship, may I bring Christ to others through the way that I live my life.

LENTEN ACTION

What characteristic that Mary exemplifies in her relationship with her Son do you most admire? Work at developing that characteristic in your own relationship with Christ.

DAY 25

Lip Service

ℬecause the spirit of the flesh very much desires and strives to have the words but cares little for the activity; it does not seek a religion and holiness in an interior spirit, but wants and desires to have a religion and a holiness outwardly apparent to people. They are the ones of whom the Lord says: *Amen, I say to you, they have received t*heir reward.

Rm 8:6

Mt 6:2

ST. FRANCIS OF ASSISI,
THE EARLIER RULE (XVII: PREACHERS), 75

A Heart Set On God

Then the word of the LORD came to me: Thus says the LORD, the God of Israel: Like these good figs, so I will regard as good the exiles from Judah, whom I have sent away from this place to the land of the Chaldeans. I will set my eyes upon them for good, and I will bring them back to this land. I will build them up, and not tear them down; I will plant them, and not pluck them up. I will give them a heart to know that I am the LORD; and they shall be my people and I will be their God, for they shall return to me with their whole heart.

JEREMIAH 24:4–7

Prayer

Lord, it is easier to speak of my faithfulness than to live it from my heart. I do not want to live a life of hypocrisy where my words say one thing but my heart and actions say another. Give me the strength and courage so that I might be a person of integrity. Permeate me with the fire of your love so that my words are not empty but reflect a heart and life devoted to you.

Lenten Action

Are there aspects of your life that do not reflect the Christian faith you profess? Take a practical step toward eliminating these aspects during the Lenten season. If necessary, seek help in doing so.

DAY 26

Reasonableness in Acts of Service and Self-Denial

*B*ut *our flesh is not bronze, nor is our strength that of stone,* rather, we are frail and inclined to every bodily weakness! I beg you, therefore, dearly beloved, to refrain wisely and prudently from an indiscreet and impossible austerity in the fasting that you have undertaken. And I beg you in the Lord to praise the Lord by your very life, to offer the Lord your *reasonable service* and your *sacrifice* always *seasoned with salt.*

Jb 6:12

Rom 12:1

Lv 2:1

ST. CLARE OF ASSISI,
"THE THIRD LETTER TO AGNES OF PRAGUE," 53

Healthy Balance in Religious Observance

Now John's disciples and the Pharisees were fasting; and people came and said to him, "Why do John's disciples and the disciples of the Pharisees fast, but your disciples do not fast?" Jesus said to them, "The wedding guests cannot fast while the bridegroom is with them, can they? As long as they have the bridegroom with them, they cannot fast. The days will come when the bridegroom is taken away from them, and then they will fast on that day.

One sabbath he was going through the grainfields; and as they made their way his disciples began to pluck heads of grain. The Pharisees said to him, "Look, why are they doing what is not lawful on the sabbath?" And he said to them, "Have you never read what David did when he and his companions were hungry and in need of food? He entered the house of God, when Abiathar was high priest, and ate the bread of the Presence, which it is not lawful for any but the priests to eat, and he gave some to his companions." Then he said to them, "The sabbath was made for humankind, and not humankind for the sabbath; so the Son of Man is lord even of the sabbath."

MARK 2:18–20, 23–28

Prayer

Lord, out of my love for you, I am often tempted to push my body too far. Help me to grow in appreciation of the goodness of my body and to show it the respect that it deserves. When I tend to overextend myself or push myself too hard, strengthen the virtue of prudence within me so that I may have a healthy attitude about acts of self-denial and service toward others.

Lenten Action

If you do not care for yourself, you can be of no good to others. When tempted to overcommit yourself, stretch yourself too thin, or be overly hard on your body, take time to care for yourself instead.

DAY 27

Sacred Spaces, Sacred People

And the Lord gave me such faith in churches that I would pray with simplicity in this way and say: "We adore You, Lord Jesus Christ, in all Your churches throughout the whole world and we bless You because by Your holy cross You have redeemed the world."

ST. FRANCIS OF ASSISI,
"THE TESTAMENT," 124–125

CHRIST IN THE ASSEMBLY OF THE CHURCH

Again, truly I tell you, if two of you agree on earth about any-thing you ask, it will be done for you by my Father in heaven. For where two or three are gathered in my name, I am there among them."

MATTHEW 18:19–20

ONE BODY IN CHRIST

I speak as to sensible people; judge for yourselves what I say. The cup of blessing that we bless, is it not a sharing in the blood of Christ? The bread that we break, is it not a sharing in the body of Christ? Because there is one bread, we who are many are one body, for we all partake of the one bread.

1 CORINTHIANS 10:15–17

PRAYER

Lord, Francis had a great respect for the sacred space of churches. While he recognized your presence throughout creation, he placed immeasurable value on his encounter with you in the Eucharist. May I too come to a deeper respect for the sacred space of your house, where you are present not only in the Eucharist, but also in the body of believers gathered in your name.

LENTEN ACTION

Make an effort to show greater reverence for the sacred space of your church. Recognize Christ's presence in the Eucharist and those gathered. Having recognized Christ's presence, not only in the Eucharist but in the body of believers, show more respect for dignity of other members of the body.

DAY 28

Growing in Virtue by Seeing Self in Mirror of Christ

Gaze upon that mirror each day,…
and continually study your face in it,
that you may adorn yourself completely,
within and without,
covered *and arrayed in needlework*   Ps 44:10
and similarly adorned   Ps 45:10-13
with the flowers and garments of all the virtues…

Indeed,
in that mirror,
blessed poverty,
holy humility,
and inexpressible charity shine forth
as, with the grace of God,
you will be able to contemplate them throughout
the entire mirror.

ST. CLARE OF ASSISI,
"THE FOURTH LETTER TO AGNES OF PRAGUE," 55

Transformation through the Image of Christ

And all of us, with unveiled faces, seeing the glory of the Lord as though reflected in a mirror, are being transformed into the same image from one degree of glory to another; for this comes from the Lord, the Spirit.

2 Corinthians 3:18

Prayer

Lord, as I gaze at your face, I see myself as you call me to be. May my heart, mind, and will be stirred to conversion by this encounter. While you serve as a mirror of me, I also desire to become a mirror that reflects your presence to the world. Assist me as I strive to become more like you by living in simplicity, humility, and love for others.

Lenten Action

Clare contemplated the face of Christ in the crucifix of the Church of San Damiano outside of Assisi. Take time to meditate before a crucifix. Study the face of Christ. How is he calling you to become more like himself? What areas of your life need transforming? Take a practical step toward transformation in one of these areas by mirroring Christ's presence to others.

Taking Up One's Cross

In what, then, can you boast? Even if you were so skillful and wise that you possessed *all knowledge,* knew how to interpret every *kind of language,* and to scrutinize heavenly matters with skill: you could not boast in these things. For, even though someone may have received from the Lord a special knowledge of the highest wisdom, one demon knew about heavenly matters and now knows more about those of earth than all human beings.

In the same way, even if you were more handsome and richer than everyone else, and even if you worked miracles so that you put demons to flight: all these things are contrary to you; nothing belongs to you; you can boast in none of these things.

But we can boast *in* our *weaknesses* and in carrying each day the holy cross of our Lord Jesus Christ.

1 Cor 13:2

1 Cor 12:28

2 Cor 12:5

Lk 14:27

ST. FRANCIS OF ASSISI,
THE ADMONITIONS (V: LET NO ONE BE PROUD
BUT BOAST IN THE CROSS OF THE LORD), 131

STRENGTH IN WEAKNESS

...Therefore, to keep me from being too elated, a thorn was given me in the flesh, a messenger of Satan to torment me, to keep me from being too elated. Three times I appealed to the Lord about this, that it would leave me, but he said to me, "My grace is sufficient for you, for power is made perfect in weakness." So, I will boast all the more gladly of my weaknesses, so that the power of Christ may dwell in me. Therefore I am content with weaknesses, insults, hardships, persecutions, and calamities for the sake of Christ; for whenever I am weak, then I am strong.

2 CORINTHIANS 12:7–10

PRAYER

Lord, you call me to follow you by taking up my own cross in life. Grant me strength and courage to more willingly and lovingly embrace the trials, struggles, and persecutions of my own life so that your glory might shine through me.

LENTEN ACTION

Adopt a more positive attitude toward the trials you face in life by uniting them with the sufferings and trials of Jesus' own life, and by reflecting upon how God's strength is made known to you and to others through the weaknesses and shortcomings you have.

Servant Leadership

I also beg that [sister] who will be in an office of the sisters to strive to exceed the others more by her virtues and holy life than by her office, so that, stimulated by her example, they obey her not so much because of her office as because of love. Let her also be farsighted and discerning toward her sisters, as a good mother is toward her daughters, and let her especially take care to provide for them according to the needs of each one out of the alms that the Lord shall give. Let her also be so kind and affable that they may securely reveal their needs and confidently have recourse to her at any hour, as they see fit both for themselves as well as for their sisters.

ST. CLARE OF ASSISI, "THE TESTAMENT," 64

THE SUFFERING SERVANT

...[H]e had no form or majesty that we should
look at him,
nothing in his appearance that we should desire him.
He was despised and rejected by others;
a man of suffering and acquainted with infirmity;
and as one from whom others hide their faces
he was despised, and we held him of no account.

Surely he has borne our infirmities
and carried our diseases;
yet we accounted him stricken,
struck down by God, and afflicted.
But he was wounded for our transgressions,
crushed for our iniquities;
upon him was the punishment that made us whole,
and by his bruises we are healed.
All we like sheep have gone astray;
we have all turned to our own way,
and the LORD has laid on him
the iniquity of us all.

He was oppressed, and he was afflicted,
yet he did not open his mouth;
like a lamb that is led to the slaughter,
and like a sheep that before its shearers is silent,
so he did not open his mouth.
Out of his anguish he shall see light;
he shall find satisfaction through his knowledge.
The righteous one, my servant, shall make many righteous,
and he shall bear their iniquities.
Therefore I will allot him a portion with the great,
and he shall divide the spoil with the strong;
because he poured out himself to death,
and was numbered with the transgressors;

yet he bore the sin of many,
and made intercession for the transgressors.

ISAIAH 53:2–7, 11–12

PRAYER

Lord, you did not lead by intimidation and fear but by loving service. Teach me that the most effective means of leadership can be found in laying down my life and becoming the servant of others. May I become the kind of leader who leads others to you.

LENTEN ACTION

Reflect on the roles of leadership that you hold, whether they be in your family, workplace, school, or community. Adapt your leadership style to better reflect that of Jesus by becoming more open, compassionate, and supportive toward those you serve.

DAY 31

Human Hesitancy to Follow Christ

$\mathcal{A}$nd He wishes all of us to be saved through Him and receive Him with our heart pure and our body chaste. But, even though His *yoke is easy* and His *burden light,* there are few who wish to receive Him and be saved through Him. Those who do not wish to taste how sweet the Lord is and who love *the darkness more than the light,* not wishing to fulfill God's commands, are cursed; it is said of them by the prophet: *Cursed are those who stray from your commands.*

Mt 11:30

Ps 34:9; Jn 3:19

Ps 119:21

St. Francis of Assisi, "Later Admonition and Exhortation
to the Brothers and Sisters of Penance," 46

The Narrow Gate

> *"In everything do to others as you would have them do to you; for this is the law and the prophets.*
>
> *"Enter through the narrow gate; for the gate is wide and the road is easy that leads to destruction, and there are many who take it. For the gate is narrow and the road is hard that leads to life, and there are few who find it.*

Matthew 7:12–14

Following Jesus by Following His Commands

Now by this we may be sure that we know him, if we obey his commandments. Whoever says, "I have come to know him," but does not obey his commandments, is a liar, and in such a person the truth does not exist; but whoever obeys his word, truly in this person the love of God has reached perfection. By this we may be sure that we are in him: whoever says, "I abide in him," ought to walk just as he walked.

1 JOHN 2:3–6

Prayer

Jesus, following you is not always easy and carefree. It does require something from me: I must follow your commands. Often, out of pride or convenience, I seek to follow my own will instead. Lead me through the narrow gate. Be merciful and soften my heart when I stubbornly refuse to follow you. Remind me that life with you is well worth any cost I may incur in following you.

Lenten Action

Pray with the Ten Commandments (Exodus 10:2–17), the Beatitudes (Matthew 5:3–11), and the great Commandment (Matthew 22:37–39). Reflect upon how your heart is slow to follow God's commands in the Hebrew Scriptures and Christ's commands in the New Testament. Work at being a more faithful disciple in these areas. When presented with the opportunity to take the easy but less ethical way out of a situation, take the more difficult route and follow Christ's commands.

DAY 32

Bearing Difficulty with Patience

*L*et them direct their attention to what they should desire above all else: to have the Spirit of the Lord and Its holy activity, to pray always to Him with a pure heart, and to have humility, patience

Mt 5:44   in difficulty and infirmity, and to love those who persecute, blame,

Mt 5:1   and accuse us, for the Lord says: *Blessed are those who suffer persecution for the sake of justice, for theirs is the kingdom of heaven.*

Mt 10:22   But *whoever perseveres to the end will be saved.*

ST. CLARE OF ASSISI, *THE FORM OF LIFE OF SAINT CLARE*
(X: THE ADMONITION AND CORRECTION OF SISTERS), 123

Empowered by God to Endure with Patience

For this reason, since the day we heard it, we have not ceased praying for you and asking that you may be filled with the knowledge of God's will in all spiritual wisdom and understanding, so that you may lead lives worthy of the Lord, fully pleasing to him, as you bear fruit in every good work and as you grow in the knowledge of God. May you be made strong with all the strength that comes from his glorious power, and may you be prepared to endure everything with patience, while joyfully giving thanks to the Father, who has enabled you to share in the inheritance of the saints in the light.

COLOSSIANS 1:9–12

Prayer

Lord, I bear many burdens in life, some of which are imposed upon me by others. There is also much that concerns me: bills, work, family, relationships, and simply how I am going to get through the day. You knew very well the tribulations of human existence. Yet you patiently accepted the shortcomings of others and the trials of life, even to the point of death. When I experience trials and worries, I often become impatient and want instant solutions to my problems. Give me strength and wisdom to be patient as I face the burdens and concerns of this life. In doing so, may I learn the wisdom that comes in trusting in you and waiting on your assistance.

Lenten Action

Work at developing the virtue of patience. When someone causes you to wait or inflicts a burden upon you, identify with the patient endurance of Christ and ask him for the strength to bear the trial patiently.

DAY 33

The Value of Silence

*L*et all the brothers be careful not to slander or engage in disputes; let them strive, instead, to keep silence whenever God gives them the grace.

ST. FRANCIS OF ASSISI, *THE EARLIER RULE*
(IX: THE BROTHERS SHOULD NOT REVILE OR DETRACT,
BUT SHOULD LOVE ONE ANOTHER), 72

And let them [the brothers in hermitages] always recite Compline of the day immediately after sunset and strive to maintain silence, recite their Hours, rise for Matins, and *seek first the kingdom of God and His justice.* And let them recite Prime at the proper hour and, after Terce, they may end their silence, ...

Mt 6:33

ST. FRANCIS OF ASSISI, "A RULE FOR HERMITAGES," 61

Woe to that [servant] who does not hold in his heart the good things the Lord reveals to him and does not reveal them by his behavior, but, under the guise of a reward, wishes instead to reveal them with his words. He receives *his reward* and his listeners carry away little fruit.

Lk 2:19, 51; Mt 6:2, 16

ST. FRANCIS OF ASSISI, *THE ADMONITIONS*
(XXI: THE FRIVOLOUS AND THE TALKATIVE RELIGIOUS), 135

SECURE IN SILENCE

For God alone my soul waits in silence,
for my hope is from him.
He alone is my rock and my salvation,
my fortress; I shall not be shaken.
On God rests my deliverance and my honor;
my mighty rock, my refuge is in God.

PSALM 62:5–7

FINDING GOD IN THE SILENCE

He said [to Elijah], "Go out and stand on the mountain before the LORD, for the LORD is about to pass by." Now there was a great wind, so strong that it was splitting mountains and breaking rocks in pieces before the LORD, but the LORD was not in the wind; and after the wind an earthquake, but the LORD was not in the earthquake; and after the earthquake a fire, but the LORD was not in the fire; and after the fire a sound of sheer silence. When Elijah heard it, he wrapped his face in his mantle and went out and stood at the entrance of the cave. Then there came a voice to him that said, "What are you doing here, Elijah?" He answered, "I have been very zealous for the LORD, the God of hosts; ..."

1 KINGS 19:11–14

PRAYER

Lord, sometimes I avoid silence out of fear of what I might hear. Help me to overcome this fear and to quiet the many noises that surround me so that I can better hear your voice in my life.

LENTEN ACTION

Do not fall into the trap of filling your life with noise. Take an opportunity to experience silence, while driving to work or doing household tasks, or simply sit in silence. Be attentive to what God says to you in the silence.

DAY 34

United in Love

*M*oreover, I admonish and exhort the sisters in the Lord Jesus Christ to *beware of all* pride, vainglory, envy, *avarice,* Lk 12:15; 21:34
care and anxiety about this world, detraction and murmuring, dis- Mt 13:22
sension and division. Let them be always eager, however, to preserve
among themselves the unity of mutual love which is the *bond of* Col 3:14
perfection.

ST. CLARE OF ASSISI,
"THE FORM OF LIFE OF SAINT CLARE," 123

LOVE ONE ANOTHER

I give you a new commandment, that you love one another. Just as I have loved you, you also should love one another. By this everyone will know that you are my disciples, if you have love for one another."

JOHN 13:34–35

PRAYER

Lord, may the example of your own life strengthen me as I seek to overcome the pride, jealousy, and backstabbing that lead to divisions between others and myself. Help me to channel the love that you have given me so that I may develop life-giving relationships with others. Unite us in our love for you and one another.

LENTEN ACTION

Express your love for another today so as to heal a wounded relationship. Work for greater unity with those around you, whether at home, work, church, or elsewhere in your community.

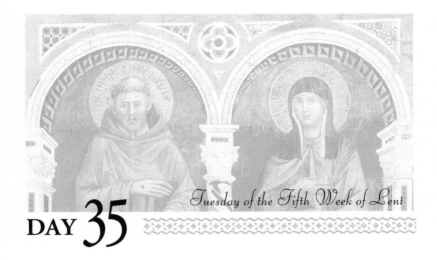

DAY 35

A New Understanding of "Friends"

Our friends, therefore, are all those who unjustly inflict upon us distress and anguish, shame and injury, sorrow and punishment, martyrdom and death. We must love them greatly for we shall possess eternal life because of what they bring us.

ST. FRANCIS OF ASSISI, *THE EARLIER RULE*
(XXII: AN ADMONITION TO THE BROTHERS), 79

Blessing Those Who Persecute Us

"But I say to you that listen, Love your enemies, do good to those who hate you, bless those who curse you, pray for those who abuse you. If anyone strikes you on the cheek, offer the other also; and from anyone who takes away your coat do not withhold even your shirt.

"If you love those who love you, what credit is that to you? For even sinners love those who love them. If you do good to those who do good to you, what credit is that to you? For even sinners do the same. But love your enemies, do good, and lend, expecting nothing in return. Your reward will be great, and you will be children of the Most High; for he is kind to the ungrateful and the wicked.

LUKE 6:27–29, 32–33, 35

Bless those who persecute you; bless and do not curse them.

ROMANS 12:14

Prayer

Jesus, given your own life experiences, you certainly understand that there are people who make life difficult for me. I ask you to change my perspective. Rather than seeing such people as a burden in life, may I see them as blessings. Lead me to an awareness of how the trials and pain that such people bring can actually lead me to you. Given my own shortcomings, teach me the wisdom of being patient with others as I surely want them to be patient with me.

Lenten Action

A wise man once said, "Never do anything deliberately to hurt someone; you will do it enough without even knowing it." When tempted to lash out at someone who aggravates you, respond with the same level of love and patience that you hope others will display toward you.

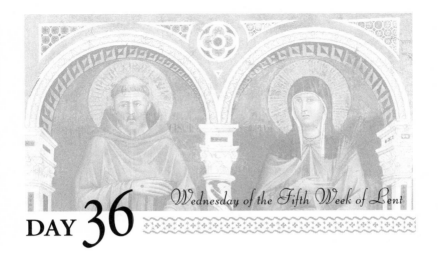

DAY 36

Strengthened for Service by Christ

...be strengthened in the holy service of the Poor Crucified
undertaken with a passionate desire,
Who *endured* the suffering of the cross — Heb 12:2
for us all,
delivering *us from the power* of the prince — Col 1:13
of darkness
to which we had been enslaved by the disobedience
of our first parent,
thus *reconciling us* to God the Father. — 2 Cor 5:18

ST. CLARE OF ASSISI,
"THE FIRST LETTER TO AGNES OF PRAGUE," 45

SERVICE IN LOVE

Above all, maintain constant love for one another, for love covers a multitude of sins. Be hospitable to one another without complaining. Like good stewards of the manifold grace of God, serve one another with whatever gift each of you has received. Whoever speaks must do so as one speaking the very words of God; whoever serves must do so with the strength that God supplies, so that God may be glorified in all things through Jesus Christ. To him belong the glory and the power forever and ever. Amen.

1 PETER 4:8–11

PRAYER

Lord Jesus, by your own example, you have shown the way to a fulfilling and authentically human life is through laying down one's life in the service of others. Inspired by your selfless example and strengthened by your Spirit, may I too give of myself in service to others and, in so doing, serve you.

LENTEN ACTION

Inspired by Jesus' example of self-giving, perform a small act of service for another person that you normally may not be expected to do. For example, take time to clean the house, pick up a child from school, or prepare a special meal when it is not our turn to cook. Do not expect any kind of recognition for the service you have performed. If you find the act of service to be difficult, ask Jesus for strength.

DAY 37

What's in a Name?

To all my reverend and dearly beloved brothers: …Brother Francis, a worthless and weak man, your very little servant sends his greetings in Him Who has redeemed and *washed us in His* most ~Rv 1:5~ precious blood. When you hear His name, the name of that *Son of* ~Lk 1:32~ *the Most High,* our Lord Jesus Christ, *Who is blessed forever,* adore ~Rm 1:25~ His name with fear and reverence, *prostrate on the ground!* ~2 Ezr 8:6~

ST. FRANCIS OF ASSISI,
"A LETTER TO THE ENTIRE ORDER," 116

Doing All in the Name of Jesus

As God's chosen ones, holy and beloved, clothe yourselves with compassion, kindness, humility, meekness, and patience. Let the word of Christ dwell in you richly; teach and admonish one another in all wisdom; and with gratitude in your hearts sing psalms, hymns, and spiritual songs to God. And whatever you do, in word or deed, do everything in the name of the Lord Jesus, giving thanks to God the Father through him.

COLOSSIANS 3:12, 16–17

Calling on the Name of God

I kept my faith, even when I said,
"I am greatly afflicted";
I said in my consternation,
"Everyone is a liar."

What shall I return to the LORD
for all his bounty to me?
I will lift up the cup of salvation
and call on the name of the LORD. . . .

PSALM 116:10–13

Prayer

Lord Jesus, hear my cry and draw near to me when I call upon your holy name. I humbly yet firmly trust that, through the power of your name, all things can be accomplished. May your name always be praised.

Lenten Action

Be careful to only use the name of the Lord with reverence. Quietly meditate while repeating the name of Jesus softly to yourself. When faced with a trial, call on and trust in the name of the Lord.

DAY 38

Forgiveness: Reconciliation With God and Neighbor

*I*f it should happen, may it never be so, that an occasion of trouble or scandal should arise between sister and sister through a word or gesture, let her who was the cause of the trouble, before offering the gift of her prayer to the Lord, not only prostrate herself humbly at once at the feet of the other and ask pardon, but also beg her simply to intercede for her to the Lord that He forgive her. Let the other sister, mindful of that word of the Lord, "If you do not *forgive* from *the heart,* neither will *your* heavenly *Father forgive you,"* generously pardon her sister every injury she has done to her.

Mt 5:23

Mt 6:15; 18:35

ST. CLARE OF ASSISI, *THE FORM OF LIFE OF SAINT CLARE*
(IX: THE PENANCE TO BE IMPOSED ON THE SISTERS WHO SIN;
THE SISTERS WHO SERVE OUTSIDE THE MONASTERY), 121–122

The Call to Unconditional Forgiveness

Then Peter came and said to him, "Lord, if another member of the church sins against me, how often should I forgive? As many as seven times?" Jesus said to him, "Not seven times, but, I tell you, seventy-seven times.

MATTHEW 18:21–22

"Do not judge, and you will not be judged; do not condemn, and you will not be condemned. Forgive, and you will be forgiven;

LUKE 6:37

Prayer

Jesus, forgiveness can be one of the toughest things to do in life. Wounds inflicted by others can pierce me deeply. Keep me mindful of your unconditional love for me so that I may be truly sorry for having offended you. As I remember your own willingness to forgive me of my failings, I ask for the inner strength to forgive those who wrong me, especially when it is most difficult.

Lenten Action

Celebrate the sacrament of reconciliation this Lent. Work at reconciliation in your life by letting go of a grudge or apologizing to someone you have hurt or offended.

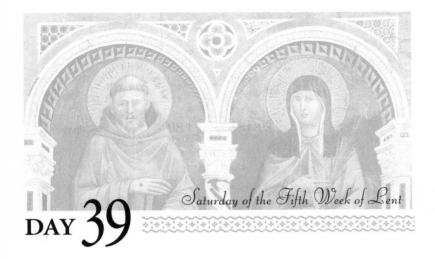

DAY 39

Trusting in God

Let the sisters not appropriate anything to themselves, neither a house nor a place nor anything at all; instead, *as pilgrims and strangers* in this world who serve the Lord in poverty and humility, let them confidently send for alms. Nor should they be ashamed, since the Lord made Himself poor in this world for us. This is that summit of the highest poverty which has established you, my dearest sisters, heiresses and queens of the kingdom of heaven; it has made you poor in things but exalted you in virtue. Let this be your portion which leads *into the land of the living.* Clinging totally to this, my most beloved sisters, do not wish to have anything else in perpetuity under heaven for the name of our Lord Jesus Christ and His most holy mother.

1 Pt 2:11

2 Cor 8:9

ST. CLARE OF ASSISI, *THE FORM OF LIFE OF SAINT CLARE*
(VIII: THE SISTERS SHALL NOT APPROPRIATE ANYTHING
AS THEIR OWN; BEGGING ALMS; THE SICK SISTERS), 119–120

The Futility of Worry

"Therefore I tell you, do not worry about your life, what you will eat or what you will drink, or about your body, what you will wear. Is not life more than food, and the body more than clothing? Look at the birds of the air; they neither sow nor reap nor gather into barns, and yet your heavenly Father feeds them. Are you not of more value than they? And can any of you by worrying add a single hour to your span of life? And why do you worry about clothing? Consider the lilies of the field, how they grow; they neither toil nor spin, yet I tell you, even Solomon in all his glory was not clothed like one of these. But if God so clothes the grass of the field, which is alive today and tomorrow is thrown into the oven, will he not much more clothe you—you of little faith? Therefore do not worry, saying, 'What will we eat?' or 'What will we drink?' or 'What will we wear?' For it is the Gentiles who strive for all these things; and indeed your heavenly Father knows that you need all these things. But strive first for the kingdom of God and his righteousness, and all these things will be given to you as well.

"So do not worry about tomorrow, for tomorrow will bring worries of its own. Today's trouble is enough for today.

MATTHEW 6:25–34

Prayer

Generous Father, St. Clare trusted that you would provide all that she and her sisters needed. Inspired by her example, and knowing that I too am in your loving hands, I turn the cares and anxieties of my life over to you and confidently trust that you will take care of all of my needs.

Lenten Action

What preoccupies your mind? Do your best to let go of this worry by placing it in God's hands and trusting it to his providence. To celebrate being freed from this concern, say or do something consoling to alleviate the worries of someone else.

DAY 40

The Love of the Cross

Look, I say, at the border of this mirror, that is,
the poverty of Him
Who was placed in a manger and
wrapped in swaddling clothes.

O marvelous humility!
O astonishing poverty!
The King of angels,
the Lord of heaven and earth,
is laid in a manger!

Lk 2:7

Then reflect upon, at the surface of the mirror,
the holy humility, at least the blessed poverty,
the untold labors and punishments
that He endured for the redemption of the whole
human race.

Finally contemplate, in the depth of this same mirror,
the ineffable charity that He chose
to suffer on the tree of the Cross
and to die there the most shameful kind of death.

St. Clare of Assisi, "The Fourth Letter
to Agnes of Prague," 56

Christ's Great Love

Who will separate us from the love of Christ? Will hardship, or distress, or persecution, or famine, or nakedness, or peril, or sword? No, in all these things we are more than conquerors through him who loved us. For I am convinced that neither death, nor life, nor angels, nor rulers, nor things present, nor things to come, nor powers, nor height, nor depth, nor anything else in all creation, will be able to separate us from the love of God in Christ Jesus our Lord.

Romans 8:35, 37–39

Prayer

Lord Jesus, you demonstrated your great love for me by all that you were willing to suffer for my sake. I cannot begin to comprehend the depths of this love. Keep me ever mindful of the great magnitude of your sacrifice. Enkindled by the fire of your love, may I too be willing to pour out my life so that I may make your love known in the world.

Lenten Action

Carry a small cross or picture of a cross with you today as a reminder of the depths of Christ's love for you. Jesus demonstrated his great love for humankind by laying down his life for others. Demonstrate your love for another person today by making some sort of sacrifice for him or her.

DAY 41

Wisdom in Simplicity

Hail, Queen Wisdom!
May the Lord protect You,
with Your Sister, holy pure Simplicity!…
Holy Wisdom confounds
Satan and all his cunning.
Pure holy Simplicity confounds
all *the wisdom of this world*
and the wisdom of the body.

1 Cor 2:6

ST. FRANCIS OF ASSISI,
"A SALUTATION OF THE VIRTUES," 164–165

The Wisdom and Simplicity of Children

At that time the disciples came to Jesus and asked, "Who is the greatest in the kingdom of heaven?" He called a child, whom he put among them, and said, "Truly I tell you, unless you change and become like children, you will never enter the kingdom of heaven. Whoever becomes humble like this child is the greatest in the kingdom of heaven.

MATTHEW 18:1–4

Prayer

Christ, I fill my life with so many activities and projects that I often make it more complicated than I need to. I further complicate my life by trying to understand and control all that is happening around me. In so doing, I distract myself from simple faith in you. Help me as I seek to unclutter my life, and teach me the wisdom of simply and unconditionally trusting you.

Lenten Action

Play with, read to, or observe a child today. What characteristics do children exhibit that you could adopt in your relationship with God? Simplify your life by cutting out an unnecessary activity.

DAY 42

Finding One's Treasure Through Humility

*T*ruly I can rejoice, and no one can rob me of such joy, since, Sg 3:4; Gn 3:1 having at last what under heaven I have desired, I see that, helped by a special gift of wisdom from the mouth of God Himself and in an awe-inspiring and unexpected way, you have brought to ruin the subtleties of our crafty enemy, the pride that destroys human nature, and the vanity that infatuates human hearts; that by humility, the virtue of faith, and the arms of poverty, you have taken hold of that *incomparable treasure hidden in the field* of the world and of the human heart, with which you have purchased that by Whom all things have been made from nothing.

ST. CLARE OF ASSISI,
"THE THIRD LETTER TO AGNES OF PRAGUE," 50

LETTING GO OF SELFISH PRIDE

If then there is any encouragement in Christ, any consolation from love, any sharing in the Spirit, any compassion and sympathy, make my joy complete: be of the same mind, having the same love, being in full accord and of one mind. Do nothing from selfish ambition or conceit, but in humility regard others as better than yourselves. Let each of you look not to your own interests, but to the interests of others.

PHILIPPIANS 2:1–4

...And all of you must clothe yourselves with humility in your dealings with one another, for "God opposes the proud, but gives grace to the humble."

Humble yourselves therefore under the mighty hand of God, so that he may exalt you in due time. Cast all your anxiety on him, because he cares for you.

1 PETER 5:5–7

PRAYER

Lord, this Lent help me let go of the pride that hinders my relationships with you and with others. Lead me out of my sense of self-sufficiency and superiority to recognize my total dependency on you. As I grow in humility, let me cling to the treasure that can be found through life with you, a treasure that the world does not begin to offer.

LENTEN ACTION

There is nothing wrong with a healthy sense of self-esteem. It is the pride that leads some people to view themselves as better than others that harms their relationship with God and with other people. Is there someone upon whom you look down? Practice developing the virtue of humility by offering praise to others and by not assuming that you are better because of your accomplishments and status in life.

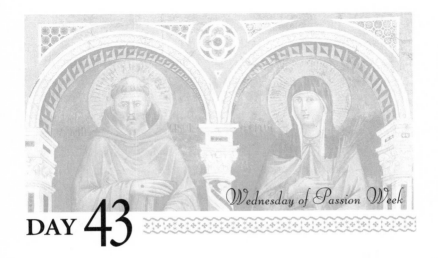

DAY 43

Balancing Spiritual Life and Work

Let the sisters to whom the Lord has given the grace of working work faithfully and devotedly . . . at work that pertains to a virtuous life and the common good. [Let them do this] in such a way that, while they banish idleness, the enemy of the soul, they do *not extinguish the Spirit* of holy prayer and devotion to which other temporal things must contribute. ^{1 Thess 5:19}

ST. CLARE OF ASSISI, *THE FORM OF LIFE OF SAINT CLARE*
(VII: THE MANNER OF WORKING), 119

PRIORITIES

Now as they went on their way, he entered a certain village, where a woman named Martha welcomed him into her home. She had a sister named Mary, who sat at the Lord's feet and listened to what he was saying. But Martha was distracted by her many tasks; so she came to him and asked, "Lord, do you not care that my sister has left me to do all the work by myself? Tell her then to help me." But the Lord answered her, "Martha, Martha, you are worried and distracted by many things; there is need of only one thing. Mary has chosen the better part, which will not be taken away from her."

LUKE 10:38–42

PRAYER

Lord, often I become so distracted by my busy life that I lose my focus on you. Teach me to keep you as the ultimate priority in my life. May my work and activities serve as means by which I am brought into deeper relationship with you.

LENTEN ACTION

Let your work become a form of prayer. While working, either at your job or at home, lift your heart and offer your work to God. Amidst your business today, take time to be mindful of God's presence in your life.

DAY 44

Laying Down Your Life

And as His Passion was near, He celebrated the Passover with His disciples and, taking bread, gave thanks, blessed and broke it, saying: *Take and eat: This is My Body.* And taking the Mt 26:26 cup He said: *This is My Blood of the New Covenant which will be poured out for you and for many for the forgiveness of sins.* Then Mt 26:28 He prayed to His Father, saying: *Father, if it can be done, let this* Lk 22:42 *cup pass from me. And His sweat became as drops of blood falling* Lk 22:44 *on the ground.* Nevertheless, He placed His will in the will of His Father, saying: *Father, let Your will be done; not as I will, but as* Mt 26:42; 26:39 *You will.* His Father's will was such that His blessed and glorious Son, Whom He gave to us and Who was born for us, should offer Himself through His own blood as a sacrifice and oblation on the altar of the cross: not for Himself through Whom all things were Jn 1:3 made, but for our sins, leaving us an example that we might follow His footprints. 1 Pt 2:21

ST. FRANCIS OF ASSISI, "LATER ADMONITION AND EXHORTATION TO THE BROTHERS AND SISTERS OF PENANCE," 46

No Greater Love

"This is my commandment, that you love one another as I have loved you. No one has greater love than this, to lay down one's life for one's friends.

JOHN 15:12–13

Prayer

Lord Jesus, giving of myself for the sake of others is one of the most difficult things to do in life, yet this is what you call me to do. At the last supper you celebrated with your friends, you showed me that this is the way to a life worth living; this is the way to a life with you. May the example of your great sacrifice and loving service to others inspire and strengthen me to lay down my own life in loving service to others.

Lenten Action

Would you be willing to give of yourself for others as radically as Jesus did? We learn to make major sacrifices in life by practicing with little ones. Demonstrate your willingness to follow Christ all the way to the cross by giving of yourself for the good of another person, if only in a small way.

Good Friday

DAY 45

Cause for Praise

Let every creature
in heaven, on earth, in the sea and in the depths,
give praise, *glory, honor and blessing*   Rv 5:13
To Him Who suffered so much,
Who has given and will give in the future every good,
for He is our power and strength,
Who *alone is good,*   Mk 10:18;
Who alone is almighty,   Lk 18:19
Who alone is omnipotent, wonderful, glorious
and Who alone is holy,
worthy of praise and blessing
through endless ages.

ST. FRANCIS OF ASSISI, "LATER ADMONITION AND EXHORTATION
TO THE BROTHERS AND SISTERS OF PENANCE," 49–50

OUR REDEMPTION

[God] destined us for adoption as his children through Jesus Christ, according to the good pleasure of his will, to the praise of his glorious grace that he freely bestowed on us in the Beloved. In him we have redemption through his blood, the forgiveness of our trespasses, according to the riches of his grace that he lavished on us. With all wisdom and insight he has made known to us the mystery of his will, according to his good pleasure that he set forth in Christ, as a plan for the fullness of time, to gather up all things in him, things in heaven and things on earth. In Christ we have also obtained an inheritance, having been destined according to the purpose of him who accomplishes all things according to his counsel and will, so that we, who were the first to set our hope on Christ, might live for the praise of his glory.

EPHESIANS 1:5–12

PRAYER

Jesus, my Savior, there are many reasons this day is "good." Today we remember how you showed your love for us, how you conquered death and suffering and won our redemption for us, and how you demonstrated that to come to life, we must first die to ourselves. Because of your sacrifice, death and suffering no longer have the final word. The victory which you won through your death is truly *good,* and I praise you for it. Today I unite my trials and sufferings with your own so that they too might become good. I ask you to continue to pour out your blessings upon me and to be my strength as I seek to be your faithful disciple all the way to the cross.

LENTEN ACTION

Christ shows us that goodness can come from suffering and loss. Make the sign of the cross while reflecting upon why this day is good for you. Give praise to God for the victory he has won and for the goodness that can come from trials and suffering in your own life.

DAY 46

Gratitude

All-powerful, most holy,
Almighty and supreme God,
Holy and just *Father,*   Jn 17:11
Lord King *of heaven and earth*   Mt 11:25
we thank You for Yourself
for through Your holy will
and through Your only Son
with the Holy Spirit
You have created everything spiritual and corporal
and, after making us *in Your own image and likeness,*
You placed us in paradise....   Gn 1:26; 2:15
We thank You
for as through Your Son You created us,
so through Your holy love
with which You loved us   Jn 17:26
You brought about His birth
as true God and true man
by the glorious, ever-virgin, most blessed, holy Mary
and You willed to redeem us captives

through His cross and blood and death.
We thank You
for Your Son Himself will come again
in the glory of His majesty…
to say to all those
who have known You, adored You and
served You in penance:
"*Come, you blessed of my Father,*
receive *the kingdom prepared for you*

Mt 25:34 from the beginning *of the world.*"

ST. FRANCIS OF ASSISI, *THE EARLIER RULE*
(XXIII: PRAYER AND THANKSGIVING), 81–82

THANKSGIVING FOR CHRIST'S VICTORY

Then the seventh angel blew his trumpet,
and there were loud voices in heaven, saying,
"The kingdom of the world has become
the kingdom of our Lord
and of his Messiah,
and he will reign forever and ever."

Then the twenty-four elders who sit on their thrones before God
fell on their faces and worshiped God, singing,
"We give you thanks, Lord God Almighty,
who are and who were,
for you have taken your great power
and begun to reign.
The nations raged,
but your wrath has come,
and the time for judging the dead,
for rewarding your servants, the prophets
and saints and all who fear your name,
both small and great,
and for destroying those who destroy the earth."

REVELATION 11:15–18

PRAYER

Lord God, I give you thanks for all of the blessings with which you have showered me: the gift of life itself, my family and friends, the beauty of creation, and all that which sustains my life. I give you thanks not only for the seemingly good things of life, but for *all* of my life, including the times of challenge, trials, and suffering. These too serve to shape me into the person you call me to be. I thank you especially for calling me to share in your Son's victory over sin and death.

LENTEN ACTION

Research has shown that thankful people are happy people. In our hectic lives, we seldom take time to truly offer God thanks for the blessings of our lives. Throughout the day, be especially mindful of all the things for which you are thankful. At the end of the day, be sure to mention in prayer at least three things for which you would like to thank God.

PART II

~~~~~

READINGS *for* EASTER

DAY 47

Let All Creation Rejoice!

Most High, all-powerful, good Lord,

Rv 4:9, 11   Yours are *the praises, the glory,* and *the honor,*
and all *blessing,*
To You alone, Most High, do they belong,
and no human is worthy to mention Your name.

Tb 8:7   Praised be You, my *Lord,* with all *Your creatures,*
especially Sir Brother Sun,
Who is the day and through whom You give us light.
And he is beautiful and radiant with great splendor;
and bears a likeness of You, Most High One.

Ps 148:3   *Praised* be You, my Lord, through Sister *Moon*
and *the stars,*
in heaven You formed them clear and precious
and beautiful.
Praised be You, my Lord, through Brother Wind,
and through the air, cloudy and serene,
and every kind of weather,
through whom You give sustenance to Your creatures.

Ps 148:4, 5   *Praised* be You, my Lord, through Sister *Water,* who is very useful and humble and precious and chaste.

Praised be You, my Lord, through Brother *Fire,* Dn 3:66

through whom *You light the night,* Ps 78:14

and he is beautiful and playful and robust and strong.

Praised be You, my Lord, through our Sister

Mother *Earth,* Dn 3:74

who sustains and governs us,

and who produces various *fruit* with colored flowers and *herbs.* Ps 104:13, 14

Praised be You, my Lord, through those

who give pardon for Your love, Mt 6:12

and bear infirmity and tribulation.

Blessed are those who endure in peace

for by You, Most High, shall they be crowned.

Praised be You, my Lord, through our Sister

Bodily Death,

from whom no one living can escape.

Woe to those who die in mortal sin.

Blessed are those whom death will find in Your most

holy will,

for *the second death* shall do them no harm. Rv 2:11; 20:6

Praise and *bless* my *Lord* and give Him thanks Dn 3:85

and serve Him with great humility.

ST. FRANCIS OF ASSISI, "CANTICLE OF THE CREATURES," 113–114

CHRIST, THE VICTOR

When this perishable body puts on imperishability,
and this mortal body puts on immortality,
then the saying that is written will be fulfilled:
"Death has been swallowed up in victory."
"Where, O death, is your victory?
Where, O death, is your sting?"
The sting of death is sin, and the power of sin is the law.
But thanks be to God, who gives us the victory
through our Lord Jesus Christ.

1 CORINTHIANS 15:54–57

PRAYER

Resurrected Lord, I join with all creation in celebrating the feast of your victory. Alleluia! The light of your resurrection gives new meaning to all of life. Death and suffering no longer have the final word. You have conquered the night and death and brought us day and life. May the joy of Easter be with me always. Renew me and fill me with your risen life as I seek to bring the good news of your resurrection to the world.

EASTER ACTION

Celebrate new life by committing yourself to environmental stewardship, social justice, and respect for the dignity of all human life.

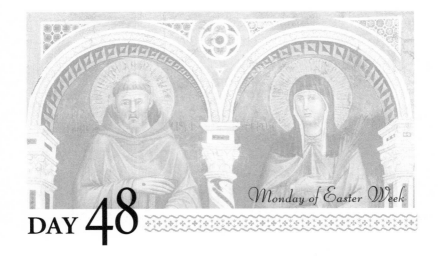

Monday of Easter Week

DAY 48

The Fleeting Nature of Things of This World

*S*ee, you blind ones, deceived by your enemies: the flesh, the world, and the devil, because it is sweet for the body to sin and it is bitter to serve God, for every vice and sin flow and *proceed from the human heart* as the Lord says in the Gospel. And you have nothing in this world or in that to come. And you think that you will possess this world's vanities for a long time, but you are deceived because a day and an hour will come of which you give no thought, which you do not know, and of which you are unaware when the body becomes weak, death approaches, and it dies a bitter death.... _{Mt 15:19; Mk 7:21}

And every talent, ability, *knowledge, and wisdom* they think they have will be taken away from them. _{2 Chr 1:12 Lk 8:18; Mk 4:25}

St. Francis of Assisi, *Earlier Exhortation to the Brothers and Sisters of Penance* (II: Those Who Do Not Do Penance), 43

WITHERING GRASS

Do not fret because of the wicked;
do not be envious of wrongdoers,

for they will soon fade like the grass,
and wither like the green herb.

Trust in the LORD, and do good;
so you will live in the land, and enjoy security.
Take delight in the LORD,
and he will give you the desires of your heart.
Commit your way to the LORD;
trust in him, and he will act.
He will make your vindication shine like the light,
and the justice of your cause like the noonday.
Be still before the LORD, and wait patiently for him;
do not fret over those who prosper in their way,
over those who carry out evil devices.

Better is a little that the righteous person has
than the abundance of many wicked.
For the arms of the wicked shall be broken,
but the LORD upholds the righteous.

PSALM 37:1–7, 16–17

PRAYER

Lord, although I might not like to think about the topic, the reality of the matter is that someday I will die. Today, as I celebrate the joy of your resurrection, I take great comfort in the knowledge that you will raise me also to new life. On that day, nothing that I have accumulated in this world, whether it be wealth, fame, power, or knowledge, will matter. Keep me mindful that all that matters now and all that will matter then is you. May knowledge of this reality shape how I view the world and all that I do and say.

EASTER ACTION

Take a moment to reflect upon what is it that you would like others to say about you when you are gone. Work at developing these traits and characteristics in your life.

DAY 49

Maintaining a Spirit of Love Amidst the Sinfulness of the World

The abbess and her sisters, however, must beware not to become angry or disturbed on account of another's sin, for anger and disturbance prevent charity in oneself and in others.

ST. CLARE OF ASSISI, *THE FORM OF LIFE OF SAINT CLARE*
(IX: THE PENANCE TO BE IMPOSED ON THE SISTERS WHO SIN;
THE SISTERS WHO SERVE OUTSIDE THE MONASTERY), 121

LOVE OVER HATRED

Hatred stirs up strife,
but love covers all offenses.

PROVERBS 10:12

WALKING IN THE LIGHT OF LOVE

Beloved, I am writing you no new commandment, but an old commandment that you have had from the beginning; the old commandment is the word that you have heard. Yet I am writing you a new commandment that is true in him and in you, because the darkness is passing away and the true light is already shining. Whoever says, "I am in the light," while hating a brother or sister, is still in the darkness. Whoever loves a brother or sister lives in the light, and in such a person there is no cause for stumbling. But whoever hates another believer is in the darkness, walks in the darkness, and does not know the way to go, because the darkness has brought on blindness.

1 JOHN 2:7–11

PRAYER

Lord of Light, help me to not despair when the darkness of the sin of the world seems overwhelming. Inspired by your own example, may I not respond to the sin of others out of hatred but out of love. Fill me with the radiance of your resurrected life and make me a light amidst the darkness that reflects your love to the world.

EASTER ACTION

What "darkness" in the world seems most threatening to you? Be a candle amidst the darkness. Take one small practical step to combat that darkness today. For example, volunteer or voice your opposition to injustice, either in conversation or in a letter to a representative or newspaper editor.

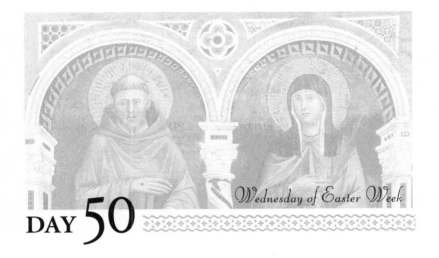

DAY 50

Sharing in the Blessings of Easter With the Communion of Saints

In the name of the Father and of the Son   Mt 28:19
and of the Holy Spirit.
May the Lord bless you and keep you.   Nm 6:24-26
May He show His face to you *and have mercy on you.*
May He turn His countenance to you and give peace to you,
my sisters and daughters, and to all others who come and
remain in your company and to others both now and in the   Mt 10:22
future...

I, Clare, a handmaid of Christ, a little plant of our most holy
father Francis, a sister and mother of you and the other poor sisters,
although unworthy, beg our Lord Jesus Christ through His mercy
and the intercession of His most holy Mother Mary and of blessed
Michael the Archangel and of all the holy angels of God, of our
blessed father Francis, and of all men and women saints, that the   Mt 5:16
heavenly Father give you and confirm for you this most holy bless-

Gn 27:28 ing in *heaven* and on *earth*: on earth, by multiplying you in grace and His virtues among His servants and handmaids in His Church Militant; in heaven, by exalting you and glorifying you among His holy men and women in His Church Triumphant.

2 Cor 1:3;
Eph 1:3 I bless you during my life and after my death, as I am able, out of all the blessings, with which *the Father of mercies* has blessed and will bless His sons and daughters *in heaven* and on earth…Amen.

ST. CLARE OF ASSISI, "THE BLESSING," 66–67

LIVING AND THE DEAD UNITED IN THE RISEN LORD

We do not live to ourselves, and we do not die to ourselves. If we live, we live to the Lord, and if we die, we die to the Lord; so then, whether we live or whether we die, we are the Lord's. For to this end Christ died and lived again, so that he might be Lord of both the dead and the living.

ROMANS 14:7–9

PRAYER

Christ, all members of your body, living and dead, are united in the joy of your resurrection. You offer all of us a share in your victory over death. May the intercession of the saints who have gone before me, including Francis and Clare and even members of my own family, bring me and all whom I love closer to you during this Easter season. Guide and strengthen me in emulating their holy lives as I continue on my own journey of faith on earth, until all members of your body are more completely united with you in the perfect joy of eternal life in heaven.

EASTER ACTION

Reflect on an aspect of the lives of Francis and Clare that you would like to incorporate into your own life. Keep a prayer card, medal, or statue of Saint Francis or Saint Clare close to you throughout the year as a reminder of your desire to become more like these saints.

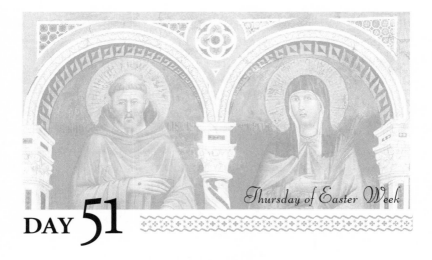

DAY 51

Gifted by God

With what eagerness and fervor of mind and body, therefore, must we keep the commandments of God and of our father, so that, with the help of the Lord, we may return to Him an increase of talents! For the Lord Himself has placed us as a model, as an example and mirror not only for others, but also for our sisters whom the Lord has called to our way of life as well, that they in turn might be a mirror and example to those living in the world. Since the Lord has called us to such great things that those who are a mirror and example to others may be reflected in us, we are greatly bound to bless and praise God and to be strengthened more and more to do good in the Lord. Therefore, if we live according to the form mentioned…, we shall leave others a noble example and gain, with very little effort, the prize of eternal happiness.

Mt 25:15-23

2 Mac 6:28, 31

Phil 3:14

ST. CLARE OF ASSISI, "THE TESTAMENT," 61

USING OUR GIFTS

And the Lord said, "Who then is the faithful and prudent manager whom his master will put in charge of his slaves, to give them their allowance of food at the proper time? Blessed is that slave whom his master will find at work when he arrives. Truly I tell you, he will put that one in charge of all his possessions. But if that slave says to himself, 'My master is delayed in coming,' and if he begins to beat the other slaves, men and women, and to eat and drink and get drunk, the master of that slave will come on a day when he does not expect him and at an hour that he does not know, and will cut him in pieces, and put him with the unfaithful. That slave who knew what his master wanted, but did not prepare himself or do what was wanted, will receive a severe beating. But the one who did not know and did what deserved a beating will receive a light beating. From everyone to whom much has been given, much will be required; and from the one to whom much has been entrusted, even more will be demanded.

LUKE 12:42–48

PRAYER

Gracious God, all belongs to you, but you have entrusted me with much. Help me to be aware of the gifts with which you have blessed me. May I show my thanks for the gifts by returning them to you in service to others.

EASTER ACTION

We don't often like to think or our own giftedness. Take time to reflect on the talents with which you have been blessed, perhaps ones you have not even noticed to this point. Find a practical way to use your talents to build up the Body of Christ, the Church.

DAY 52

Rejoicing in God's Victory

*W*ho is there, then, who would not encourage me to rejoice over such marvelous joys? Therefore, dearly beloved, may you too *always rejoice in the Lord.* And may neither bitterness nor Phil 4:4; 4:1 a cloud overwhelm you...

ST. CLARE OF ASSISI,
"THE THIRD LETTER TO AGNES OF PRAGUE," 51

THE JOY OF THE WOMEN AT THE TOMB

After the sabbath, as the first day of the week was dawning, Mary Magdalene and the other Mary went to see the tomb. And suddenly there was a great earthquake; for an angel of the Lord, descending from heaven, came and rolled back the stone and sat on it. His appearance was like lightning, and his clothing white as snow. For fear of him the guards shook and became like dead men. But the angel said to the women, "Do not be afraid; I know that you are looking for Jesus who was crucified. He is not here; for he has been raised, as he said. Come, see the place where he lay. Then go quickly and tell his disciples, 'He has been raised from the dead, and indeed he is going ahead of you to Galilee; there you will see him.' This is my message for you." So they left the tomb quickly with fear and great joy, and ran to tell his disciples.

MATTHEW 28:1–8

PRAYER

Lord, during this season celebrating your victory over all sin, suffering, and death, fill me with your Spirit of joy so that I need not succumb to the sometimes overwhelming worries, troubles, and woes of the world.

EASTER ACTION

Do something to share the joy of the victory of the Easter season with others. For example, offer an encouraging word to someone who may need a boost, or take time to enjoy a recreational activity with family or friends.

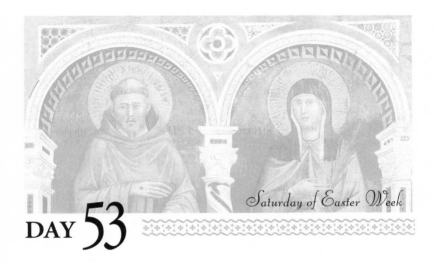

DAY 53

Brought to Life in the Glory of Christ

Happy, indeed, is she
to whom it is given to drink at this sacred banquet
so that she might cling with her whole heart to Him
Whose beauty all the blessed hosts of heaven
unceasingly admire,
Whose tenderness touches,
Whose contemplation refreshes,
Whose kindness overflows,
Whose delight overwhelms,
Whose remembrance delightfully dawns,
Whose fragrance brings the dead to life again,
Whose glorious vision will bring happiness
to all the citizens of the heavenly Jerusalem,
which [vision],   Heb 1:3
since He is the radiance of eternal *glory*   Wis 7:26
    is *the brightness of eternal light and*
    the mirror without blemish.

ST. CLARE OF ASSISI,
"THE FOURTH LETTER TO AGNES OF PRAGUE," 54–55

WE SHALL BE RAISED TO NEW LIFE

If the Spirit of him who raised Jesus from the dead dwells in you, he who raised Christ from the dead will give life to your mortal bodies also through his Spirit that dwells in you.

ROMANS 8:11

Then Jesus said to them, "Very truly, I tell you, it was not Moses who gave you the bread from heaven, but it is my Father who gives you the true bread from heaven. For the bread of God is that which comes down from heaven and gives life to the world." They said to him, "Sir, give us this bread always."

Jesus said to them, "I am the bread of life. Whoever comes to me will never be hungry, and whoever believes in me will never be thirsty. And this is the will of him who sent me, that I should lose nothing of all that he has given me, but raise it up on the last day. This is indeed the will of my Father, that all who see the Son and believe in him may have eternal life; and I will raise them up on the last day."

JOHN 6:32–35, 39–40

PRAYER

Risen Christ of glory, you are the source of all that is good, true, pleasing, and beautiful in the world. Having conquered death through your resurrection, you continue to give life to all those who place their faith in you. Let me share in your risen life, both in this world and in the world to come.

EASTER ACTION

Look for signs of the new life of spring in nature. Bring flowers into your home as a reminder of this new life. Reflect upon the beauty of nature and how it is a reflection of God's own goodness and beauty.

DAY 54

Witnessing to Christ

*L*isten, sons of the Lord and my brothers, *pay attention to my words. Incline the ear* of your heart and obey the voice of the Son of God. Observe His commands with your whole heart and fulfill His counsels with a perfect mind. *Give praise* to Him *because He is good; exalt* Him *by your deeds;* for this reason He has sent you into the whole world: that you may bear witness to His voice in word and deed and bring everyone to know that there is *no one who is all-powerful* except Him. Persevere *in discipline* and holy obedience and, with a good and firm purpose, fulfill what you have promised Him. The Lord *God* offers *Himself* to us as to His *children.*

Acts 2:14;
Is 55:3

Ps 136:1

Tb 13:6

Tb 13:4;
Heb 12:7

Heb 12:7

ST. FRANCIS OF ASSISI,
"A LETTER TO THE ENTIRE ORDER," 116–117

Bringing Christ to the Ends of the Earth

Now the eleven disciples went to Galilee, to the mountain to which Jesus had directed them. When they saw him, they worshiped him; but some doubted. And Jesus came and said to them, "All authority in heaven and on earth has been given to me. Go therefore and make disciples of all nations, baptizing them in the name of the Father and of the Son and of the Holy Spirit, and teaching them to obey everything that I have commanded you. And remember, I am with you always, to the end of the age."

MATTHEW 28:16–20

Prayer

Christ, through these past days of Lent and Easter, I have entered into the sorrows of death but have also risen to the joys of new life with you. Fill me with your Spirit so that I may remain faithful to you. Help me to share, through word and deed, what I have gained this Lent and Easter with all whom I encounter.

Easter Action

Often we feel awkward in sharing with others the good news of the life we have received through our relationship with Christ. As you continue through the Easter season and the coming year, vow to overcome your hesitancy to share Christ with others through word and deed.